LED BY THE LAND
LANDSCAPES BY KIM WILKIE

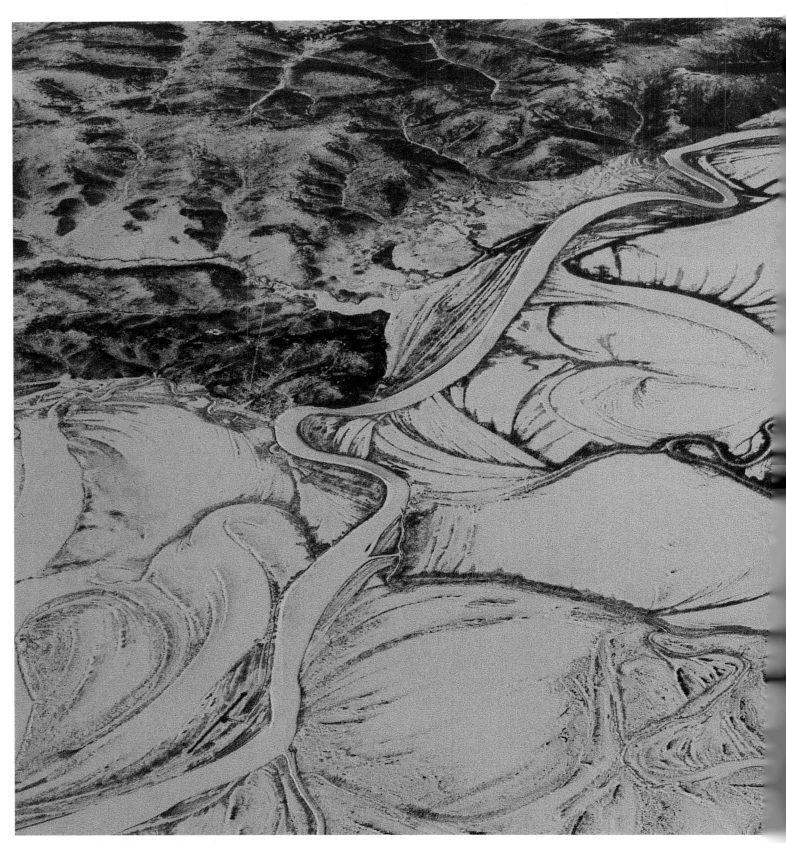

Meandering and braided rivers of ice in Canada.

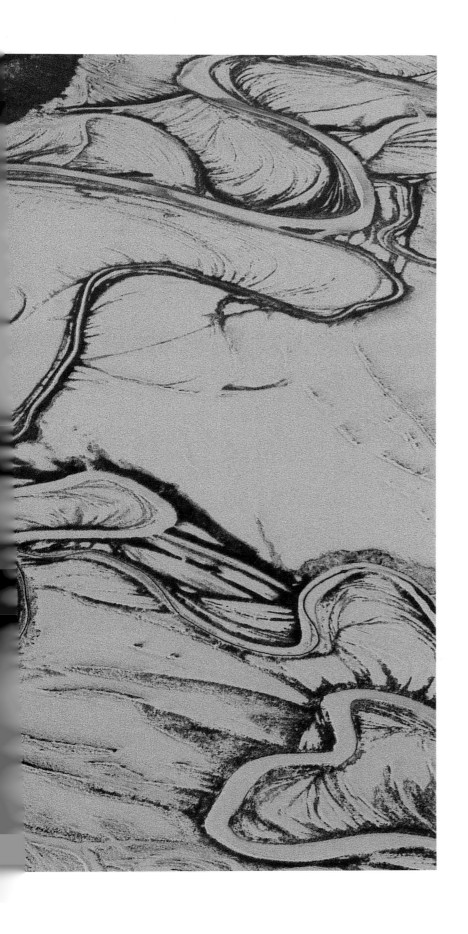

LED BY THE LAND

LANDSCAPES BY KIM WILKIE

F

FRANCES LINCOLN LIMITED
PUBLISHERS

Frances Lincoln Limited
4 Torriano Mews
Torriano Avenue
London NW5 2RZ
www.franceslincoln.com

Led by the Land
Copyright © Frances Lincoln Limited 2012
Text copyright © Kim Wilkie 2012
Illustrations and photographs © Kim Wilkie, except those
credited on page 176

First Frances Lincoln edition 2012

A catalogue record for this book is available
from the British Library.

978-0-7112-3325-6

Printed and bound in China

9 8 7 6 5 4 3 2 1

Designed by Becky Clarke

Orpheus at Boughton.

CONTENTS

Franklin Farm, Hampshire.

We used to live in a house on stilts on the edge of the jungle. There was no glass in the windows, just heavy, slatted shutters that we scrambled to close when a tropical storm broke. Lavatory paper had to be locked away because the monkeys loved to swing through the house, scoop up the rolls and festoon them through the treetops. There were umbrellas of bamboo and waxed paper furled in the corridors to protect us from the fruit bats that flew through the house, loosing bombs of bright liquid.

It was a childhood of intense images: butterflies, orchids, cowries and temples – dense with colour and smell. Things decayed as fast as they grew. Climbing plants felt as though they could scale a house overnight, covering the meagre man-made things inside that rotted as rapidly as the vines grew. Leather shoes would fur over with a pale blue mould in hours and SAS ants would carry off any food left unguarded. This was nature at its most mischievous. It had pace.

From Malaysia we moved to Iraq. The desert was complete peace; it felt slow and pale and eternal. The sky was huge and the stars seemed to ricochet across the horizon. Nothing rotted and it never seemed to rain. We spent the winter out in the desert looking for traces of former lives where Mesopotamian cities can be picked out as abandoned mounds in the sand. We walked slowly over the surface searching for fragments from millennia ago. As the wind scoured the surface, it would reveal a Roman coin, a Phoenician glass bead or the corner of a tablet with cuneiform script. It took great concentration to distinguish dusty artefact from eroded rock and sand. Everything was brown. Sometimes you could stare at a patch of ground for hours and not see the suggestive shape that marked the ear of a little figurine or iridescence of a shard of glass from a tear vase. Then when it suddenly came into focus, the ground became the secret guardian of ancient treasure. You could touch a handle that someone had grasped 5,000 years ago, just lying there exposed on the surface of the desert.

Those extremes of land, water and human occupation gave me a vivid sense of landscape. From typhoons to sand storms, violent weather held a thrill. I remember staring from our little bungalow in Sek Kong for two days as Typhoon Wanda ripped off our neighbours' roofs and hurled boats inland. I was watching from the protection of childhood, where flying roofs looked like magic and monsoon drains became water flumes that my sister and I could ride down the valley. Violent weather now commands more respect.

Coming to England was another kind of shock. We arrived in the Big Freeze of 1962, one of the coldest winters on record in the United Kingdom. My parents rented a house without central heating and then, after a year, left me in a boarding school that was equally casual about the cold. My picture of the world formed within that triangle of climates and cultures. In Malaysia I wallowed in mud; in Iraq I carved miniature cities out of cliffs of compacted sand; and in England I learned to grow plants. But perhaps most significant of all was the long-term reaction to a nomadic early life. When we finally settled on a small farm in Hampshire, I put down a taproot that tethers deep.

I didn't discover landscape architecture until I was twenty-one and in my last year of a degree in modern history at Oxford. It came as a thunderbolt. I could hardly believe that everything I loved could be wrapped up in one profession: people, land, biology and drawing. I have been led on from there.

INTRODUCTION

For something so rooted, our perception of landscape is surprisingly fluid. Landscape is a kind of riddle: it changes with every cloud and mood, yet it is timeless and stationary. In a way landscape is an endless conversation between the immensity of the geologic crust of the Earth and the bubbling lives lived and shaped upon it. To understand landscape, you need to follow the natural flows of land, water, climate and people and the accumulated memories and associations that swirl around in each place.

When it comes to trying to work with landscape, the task can be as much about ideas and attitudes as physical form. Landscape architecture essentially deals with a trinity of land, life and the stories each tells about the other. The key is to listen to the stories and then continue the tale, allowing the memory and imagination of what has gone before to inspire fresh design in the evolving pattern.

The landscape historian Mavis Batey introduced me to the subtleties of Alexander Pope and the clarity of his ideas about landscape. Pope completely understood that landscape is as much about poetry as it is about design. But more importantly he grasped the essential practicalities of surviving on the land. In his fourth epistle to Burlington in 1731 he wrote: 'All must be adapted to the Genius and the Use of the Place, and the Beauties not forced into it, but resulting from it.' The 'Genius of the Place' has become something of a catch phrase to cover the intrinsic character and personality of a place; but the 'Use' bit is usually forgotten. Pope was stressing that how we live on the land – the need to interact with food, water and shelter – is as critical to design as how we feel about it. Landscape architecture has real responsibility for how we use land and natural resources. It is not art, though it should be artful.

The eighteenth-century English Enlightenment was a scientific and philosophical shift that plunged humans into the centre of nature rather than allowing them an elegant separation from the natural world behind baroque patterns and divine benediction. It was the moment, at a new distance from the Abrahamic faiths, when magic met science. The combination of Isaac Newton and Alexander Pope was potent. Pope revived the classical nature gods of the Renaissance as a mystical metaphor and revealed beauty in well-farmed land. The Augustan poets had returned with sharp science in their ink. The basic operations of human existence were to be acknowledged and enjoyed as part of life and landscape. The view out from the garden into the productive countryside became as important as the elegant garden itself. Horace Walpole, sitting on his terrace sipping sherbet at Strawberry Hill, enjoyed the vista down the river to Twickenham as an essential part of his carefully constructed landscape. Twickenham was his 'seaport in miniature' and watching people toiling at the quays put the gloss on his own leisurely relaxation. The animation of the prospect was everything. Landscape was recognized as movement, life and interaction rather than a static and enclosed idealization of heavenly patterns.

The Enlightenment appreciation of landscape has come and gone over the centuries, but it feels particularly relevant now that we appear to be at a turning point. Abrupt and radical shifts in climate, finance and politics have unsettled our view of the world and its future. Together, they make an alarming mix. On the positive side, while we in the West have been relatively comfortable and untroubled, there has been little incentive to change the way we live. Although concern about climate change has been temporarily overwhelmed by worries about money and politics, our assumptions

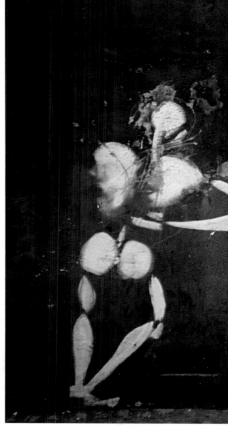

Grafitti, Rome.

about growth and the way that we survive on the planet are all now freshly challenged. The debate needs to develop beyond carbon to the way that we actually live. We have a chance to question some of the twentieth-century fundamentals of economics. Is it possible, for example, to pursue growth in fulfilment rather than growth in accumulation? Can we channel our energy into improving the quality of our lives rather than increasing the quantity of our possessions?

In the twists and turns of justice and politics, landscape architecture has a few insistent issues to raise, such as food and water. Some sort of sensible stewardship of the land has to be at the basis of any political and financial solution. How can we grow our food? Where will the water come from? What sort of buildings should be built and where? How do we cohabit with one another and nature? Can we hold on to the wit and spirit of what has gone before and let it inspire new ideas and design?

These questions are the basics of landscape architecture and this book tries to look at some of the issues raised in the work that I have done over the last couple of decades. It starts with land and water. The sacred Russian monastery of Solovki presents life on the edge of existence. For 5,000 years human civilization has managed to cling on to the rim of the Arctic Circle, delicately gathering food, light and inspiration in a place where humans struggle to survive each winter. It is a place of brutality and belief. The Saxon villages of Transylvania work on the same careful principles of stewardship, but face a more uncertain political and economic future. These are places of magical and monstrous histories that show how mere survival can determine landscape, buildings and beliefs.

Back in England, the Thames Landscape Strategy makes a striking contrast, exploring the evolution of a rich, fertile river valley and its ability to infuse a culture and an empire. It links to a repeating Arcadian idyll that, in varying shades, has obsessed the Augustan poets of Rome, the Florentine Renaissance, the English Enlightenment and the twentieth-century return to the land. My projects at Villa La Pietra in Florence, the Oxford and Moscow Botanic Gardens, the Chelsea Barracks in London and Longwood Gardens in Pennsylvania explore these ideas.

From land and water, we move to life: wild and human. Wet meadows around Winchester demonstrate the relationship between land, water, food and wildlife. The chalk streams of Hampshire provide some of the rarer habitats in the world and through these I show how landownership, recreation and design can combine to create a lively landscape of arrested adolescence. I then turn to urban life with projects at the Victoria and Albert Museum, the war memorials of Hyde Park Corner, the community garden of Hyde Abbey, and finally ideas for burying the dead in the City of London Cemetery.

The third part of the book concentrates on the spirit of design and the way it can link back to long traditions and the retelling of stories. I explore a personal obsession with landform and the many ways that you can carve and mould the earth. Inspirations come from the deeply English tradition of major earthworks from Iron Age forts, such as Maiden Castle, to the land sculptures of Charles Bridgeman and John Aislabie, and through to the magical works of Andy Goldsworthy. These have helped set my ideas racing for projects from Heveningham Hall in Suffolk through to Holker Hall in Cumbria and Boughton in Northamptonshire.

Finally I look at my own home ground and how the place has shaped the way I live and design.

Dried riverbed, Utah.

LAND AND WATER

In the total volume of the planet, we inhabit the thinnest layer on the surface of the sphere and rely on a meagre band of atmosphere that hovers above that layer. The cross-section through the Earth is 12,756 kilometres (7,926 miles), but the habitable crust is only 50 kilometres (31 miles) and the atmosphere is less than 12 kilometres (7 miles) high. This places life in a very fragile band around the planet. Landscape architecture has to start here, in this extraordinary film of biosphere. Landscape is our physical and cultural relationship with land, water and air.

ON THE EDGE

To throw that relationship into sharpest relief, I look here at some of the extremes of human existence. Life on the edge of climate comfort leaves little room for manoeuvre. Just securing food and shelter gives an acute awareness of the importance of land and water. It is revealing to see how settlements survive under these conditions and it emphasizes where landscape architecture needs to begin. It also highlights where our priorities might lie as climate change accelerates. Over the years I have worked on a few projects that have shown great ingenuity in basic survival and long-term stewardship of the land. Two in particular – the Solovki Archipelago and the Saxon villages of Transylvania – give insights into the way that we might look at the principles of settlement afresh.

SOLOVKI
RUSSIA

LEFT The Solovetsky Archipelago sits in the White Sea on the edge of the Arctic Circle. Great Muksalma Island is linked by a causeway to the main Bolshoi Solovetsky Island.

BELOW The Solovki Transfiguration Cathedral built 1556–66 and recently restored after the destruction of the Gulag occupation. The monastery is one of the most sacred in Russia and was founded in 1436 by Saints Savvatii and Zosima.

The Solovetsky Archipelago has formed at the junction of tectonic plates in the White Sea on the edge of the Russian Arctic Circle. The Earth's crust is unusually thin at this point and geothermal heat reaches the surface, contributing to a microclimate that has helped humans to inhabit the remote islands for at least five thousand years. It is a place of spiritual intensity. Over the millennia, people have shown their veneration with structures from early pagan stone labyrinths to one of the most sacred of the Russian monasteries. Solovki was also the first labour camp in the Soviet Gulag and a place of murder and torture.

The journey to the archipelago is most possible in summer when the sea has thawed from a wreckage of ice cliffs and crevasses to milky water, allowing boats to cross from the port of Kem on the Russian mainland. Even in summer it is not an easy journey. The train from Moscow to Kem takes twenty-five hours and the port is a grim, abandoned

RIGHT The small wooden church of St Andrew, built by Peter the Great in 1702 on Great Zayatsky Island.

BELOW The seventeenth-century causeway to Muksalma. The sinuous design acts as a breakwater, creating protected pockets for farming fish.

place of rusting metal. The small boat that sets out towards the Arctic Circle seems to be heading off the edge of the world. Then, just as you think you'll never see land again, a tiny globe floats on the horizon. Slowly the globe rises out of the water on a white tower. More globes and towers gradually appear and finally the monastery becomes visible, balancing on a spit between the harbour and the Holy Lake. It seems to emerge straight from the water.

Solovki embodies life on the edge. In the fragile environment of the Far North the monks evolved a system of land management from the fifteenth-century onwards that was balanced on the limit of survival. They experimented with growing and storing sufficient food and fuel in summer to last them through the six months of dark isolation during the Arctic winter. They managed to drain enough bogs, to grow enough hay, to support enough cattle, to produce enough manure, to fertilize enough vegetables, to survive. They knew just how much seaweed they could harvest without upsetting the micro-environment around the shore and they banned any logging of trees, allowing only collection of fallen dry wood for fuel. A small botanical garden was grown for medicines and for bees, as much to provide wax for candles and winter light as for honey.

The monastery was not just a place of primitive subsistence; it became a religious and cultural focus of great significance. It was also a place of technology and innovation, constantly refining land management with engineering sophistication while at the same time retaining a careful balance with natural systems. The network of fifty lakes, into which the bogs were drained, were in turn linked by canals to provide a flow of pure drinking water and ultimately hydroelectric power to the monastery. Even the causeways connecting the islands were designed as hydrodynamic forms to moderate ocean currents for fish farming.

Solovki was much destroyed during the Soviet period and the brutal passage through the Gulag, but the monks have now returned and the archipelago has been recognized as a World Heritage site. I was commissioned by the Prince of Wales's Business Leaders Forum to provide initial advice on how to restore and sustain the historic cultural landscape. In many ways this project epitomizes the relationship between man, land and fragile cultural existence. I worked with the Russian botantist Artyom Parshin, and my role as landscape architect was initially a kind of triage:

The ice house used for preserving food in summer in the vegetable garden beside the Archimandrite's hermitage.

to identify what was most significant, most vulnerable and most urgent to restore and repair. It was a delicate balancing of political, cultural and natural priorities. There were sensitive questions, such as which twentieth-century buildings should be removed to reveal the monastery in its dramatic setting without distorting some of the darker history of the place, and how new facilities could be included without destroying the harmony of the whole. Furthermore the future of the World Heritage site, and indeed the monastery community, depend on a viable economic solution. There are difficult decisions to be made about the numbers and types of visitors, residents and pilgrims allowed to travel to the

archipelago, weighing income and public access against impact on the natural and cultural environment. As a start, in such a complex web of jurisdictions, expectations and funding sources, I tried to capture the essences of the place in a brief analysis that could stir the imagination and focus priorities.

LEFT Many of the 1950s buildings beyond
the monastery are now empty and
redundant. Their removal would help to
repair the wild setting of the sixteenth-
century cathedral complex and restore its
relationship with the White Sea.

ABOVE One of the Neolithic labyrinths
that still survive on Great Zayatsky
Island. Solovki has been a sacred site for
thousands of years.

TRANSYLVANIA
ROMANIA

The work in Solovki led on to a similar project for another World Heritage site, the Siebenburgen in Transylvania for the Mihai Eminescu Trust and the Prince of Wales's Charitable Foundation. The Siebenburgen are a group of Saxon villages in the centre of Romania. A story goes that when the Pied Piper of Hamelin led the children out of rat-infested Hamburg he brought them to a new life in Transylvania. More prosaically, Lower Rhinelanders were invited by the Hungarian King Geza II in the twelfth century to colonize the south-eastern frontier of his country as a buffer zone against the invading Ottomans. These 'Saxons' were granted land and virtual autonomy by King Geza and they quickly established 200 villages in the area.

The Saxon villages, community and way of life have changed remarkably little since the twelfth century, despite a rather violent and turbulent history. From 1241 onwards, the settlers faced raids by Mongols, Ottomans, Hungarians and Romanians as well as the plague. After the Second World War the majority of the adult Saxon population was sentenced to seven years' hard labour in the Soviet Union and only about half of the deported Saxons survived to return to a communist Romania. Then in 1990, following Ceausescu's removal from power, the Saxons were invited to repatriate to Germany seven centuries after their original departure. There was a mass emigration, leaving the future of the villages very uncertain.

Astonishingly the Saxon villages still just manage to survive as the closest thing to a medieval landscape in Europe. There is the remnant of a beautiful balance between settlement, cultivation and nature. In the gentle, rolling countryside, the villages are tucked economically into the valley folds and defensible, fortified church complexes stand at strategic highpoints. Symmetrical patterns of terraced street houses, cobbled courtyards and wooden barns extend in strips up the valley sides through vegetable gardens, orchards and meadows to thickly wooded ridges. Everywhere there are animals: horses, cows, pigs and poultry in the villages; wolves, bears, lynx and wild boar in the forests; and eagles, owls, storks and larks in the skies. The meadows are lush with wild

The Saxon villages of Transylvania survive in medieval harmony with the land. Agriculture, wildflowers, farm animals, wildlife and humans are all mutually dependent.

The villages are tucked economically into the folds of the land, facing on to an animal-dominated main street. Narrow street frontages open back to long parcels that rise through courtyards, stables, vegetable gardens, orchards and vineyards to the pasture and woods beyond. The village community is concentrated on the street and each plot relates equally up to the valley sides.

The villages are a model of sustainable rural settlement, but the life is hard and the population ageing and thinning.

flowers and streams run fresh from hillside springs. The rhythm of grazing, hay and harvesting sets the pace of life. Each dawn in Viscri a young boy leads the village cattle out to pasture and the courtyard doors of the houses open for their cows to follow him in single file down the street. In the evening he returns and each cow peels off nonchalantly to her respective address, as the villagers welcome them back with a shot of local vodka. It is the kind of harmony of human settlement in nature that we can only dream about in the twenty-first century.

Since the 1990 exodus, the villages have emptied and the remaining communities are mostly elderly and impoverished. This, combined with Romania's entry into the European Union, the Common Agricultural Policy and the disbanding of the collective farms and acquisition of large swathes of fertile land by foreign investors, means that the traditional labour-intensive methods of farming are becoming more and more tenuous. But most of all, the remnant population of the Saxon villages clearly wants to rise out of subsistence farming to enjoy the benefits of modern life.

My task was again to follow a triage of landscape assessment of the most significant, vulnerable and viable. I then had to help communicate a wider understanding of the unique value of the place. I was also asked to make suggestions for the full and healthy development of the communities that are an intrinsic part of the character and management of the landscape. The process was similar to that at Solovki, but the landscape is fundamentally different. In Transylvania it is the typical as

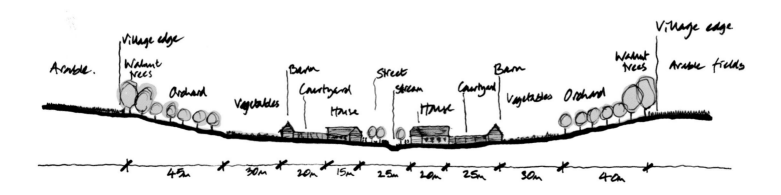

much as the unique that is significant. It is the consistent pattern of settlements in the landscape that is special, rather than individual flourishes. Most precious of all is the way of life, where centuries of careful management of the land and woods have led to a remarkable interaction of habitats. Human and wild life are completely interdependent. The wildflower meadows would revert to forest if they were not cut and harvested each year. The rich flora of the woods would be shaded out if the processes of thinning and coppicing were to stop. The complex ties of the community would be fundamentally changed if the shared and pervasive management of the land were to be transferred to a mechanized third party. Keeping some form of labour-intensive agriculture is the key to the survival of the remarkable landscape, as well as employment and community. The challenge is to stimulate sufficient local and specialist markets to keep farming viable, to use mechanization at a scale that does not destroy the land and to encourage the young to return to the villages.

There is no simple way to catapult the twelfth century into the twenty-first, keeping the best and leapfrogging the mistakes. Although it might feel as though Transylvania holds some magic recipe for the Arcadian ideal of living with the land, few of us would put up with the severity of that existence. The Mihai Eminescu Trust Whole Village Project tries to link every aspect of the community's survival. It is largely run and organized by leading figures within the local community and addresses everything from healthcare and education to infrastructure and legal and political protection. Our contribution was to attempt to highlight the most important and fragile aspects of the landscape and natural environment, while at the same time finding sensitive and economic ways of introducing running water, local natural sewage treatment, cooperative agriculture ventures, internet connections, outside funding possibilities and sympathetic architectural conservation. In almost every project the key is to help people to see and choose what is special and then to explore ways in which those priorities might be achieved in the simplest, most straightforward and sensitive steps.

The agricultural methods have changed little since the Middle Ages and the wildflower hay meadows are some of the best in Europe. The challenge is to introduce mechanization in a way that makes life easier without destroying the soil structure and floral diversity that creates a landscape which is beautiful, productive and full of life.

WATER

The relentless persistence of water has created most of the landscapes we inhabit. It has eroded mountains, carved valleys and meandered at will across plains. Water sculpts the form of the land from the raw material of geology. More gently, water also makes settlement possible in the landscapes it creates. Fresh water for drinking and irrigation, and coastal and river water for transport and defence, have determined the location of most towns and cities. London is a perfect example.

The River Thames lies at the physical and spiritual centre of London. The flow of water through the capital is a powerful natural force that links the city westwards to the centre of England and eastwards to the sea; it is London's original reason for being. The daily tidal rhythm dramatically changes the shape and size of the river hour by hour. As well as bringing light, space and wildlife into the centre of the city, it offers a menacing reminder that flood and drought lurk as sudden possibilities. London has less per capita annual rainfall than Israel, but if the Tidal Barrier were to fail the central corridor of the city could be flooded, threatening 1.25 million people, 400 schools, 16 hospitals, 13 mainline stations, 8 power stations and much of the Underground system.

The river changes character through London. From the estuary in the east, the marshes and industrial areas give way to docklands upstream of the Tidal Barrier. In the centre between Tower and Chelsea Bridges, the city is denser but it turns greener and more residential towards Kew. Between Kew and Hampton the Thames meanders through a unique landscape of parks, palaces and working communities.

The Thames Valley at Richmond was the cradle of the English Landscape Movement in the eighteenth century. With apparent mutual respect and affection the wife and mistress of George II – Queen Caroline and Henrietta Howard – living on opposite banks of the river – joined forces to patronize a radical new landscape philosophy. They befriended and employed the leading landscape architects and thinkers of the time: Alexander Pope, Charles Bridgeman, William Kent and Lancelot Brown. Their projects along this stretch of the Thames set the pattern for a more natural and fluid appreciation of landscape. Views and vistas were carefully merged to create a pastoral landscape where garden, river, man and beast were part of a seamless whole. Alexander Pope was writing and experimenting on his own garden at Twickenham and, just after Pope's death, Horace Walpole began on Strawberry Hill, within sight of Pope's villa.

The pattern of development of London has been largely determined by the geology and hydrology of the Thames. People instinctively relate to the river landscape and planning policy needs to look a hundred years ahead, while understanding the logical complexity of centuries of settlement behind.

I became involved with this upper Arcadian stretch of the river over twenty years ago. It all started with a 'Thames Connections' exhibition by the Royal Fine Art Commission in 1991. They invited nine young architects and a landscape architect to come up with ideas for the river. Rather than look at a specific building project, I became fascinated by a bird's-eye view of the whole river and its interaction with the city. By looking at historic maps and paintings, it was possible to trace the way that the upstream section of the London Thames was linked by ancient sightlines and vistas that worked with the topography of the land and the bends in the river. The form of the land, the flow of the water and strategic sightlines have shaped the character and development of this part of London.

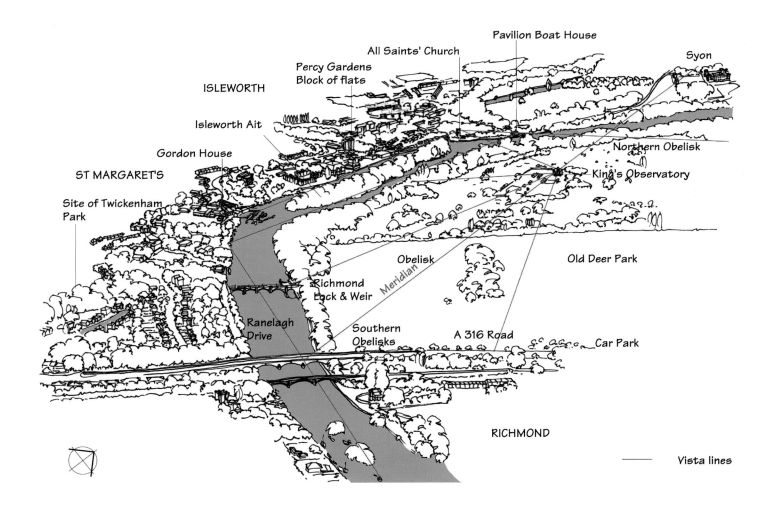

LEFT ABOVE *Richmond Hill, on the Prince Regent's Birthday*, by Joseph Mallord William Turner, exhibited 1819.

LEFT BELOW The view from Richmond Hill protected by Act of Parliament in 1902 and restored as wildflower meadow in 2005.

BELOW Syon House from Kew Gardens. The two estates were designed by Lancelot Brown to flow visually together and the grazed wet meadow beside the river is now a Site of Special Scientific Interest.

An extraordinary sequence of views still survives that stretches right across London, linking Windsor Castle to a Neolithic barrow on the top of Richmond Hill to St Paul's Cathedral to Greenwich. More locally, a network of sightlines along avenues and mounts connected all the palaces and major houses in the first 18 kilometres (11 miles) of the city from Hampton Court Palace to Kew. The rhythm of open space and working waterfronts that was established around these natural factors, views and landownerships still sets the pattern of urban design today.

The exhibition provoked some interest in south-west London and members of the local community approached me to take the ideas further. Over a period of three years, with the help of a remarkable range of inspired and dedicated people, we managed to prepare the *Thames Landscape Strategy: Hampton to Kew*. It was a rather different way of looking at planning a city. Instead of analysing the place in terms of specialist layers of zoning, we explored the river landscape as a whole: what it looks and feels like and how

The *Thames Landscape Strategy, Hampton to Kew* frames policies that respond to the way that people experience and understand the city around the river. The words and the plans try to be as approachable as possible.

BRENTFORD

Sheen Museum Tower

St George's Church

Grand Union Canal

Kew Palace

Royal Botanic Gardens

KEW

Palm House

Syon

ISLEWORTH

Pavilion

All Saints' Church

Pagoda

King's Observatory

Richmond Lock

Richmond Palace

RICHMOND

St Matthias' Church

Richmond Hill

Star and Garter

Marble Hill

York House

Orleans House

St Mary's Church

TWICKENHAM

Ham House

Henry VIII's Mound

Pembroke Lodge

Pope's Grotto

Radnor Gardens

Strawberry Hill

HAM

Ham Common

Richmond Park

Parkgate House

Teddington Weir

St Alban's Church

TEDDINGTON

Upper Lodge

Bushy Park

KINGSTON

Garrick's Villa

All Saints' Church

Hogsmill River

Hampton Court Palace

St Paul's Church

St Raphael's Church

EAST MOLESEY

SURBITON

Seething Wells Pump House

THAMES DITTON

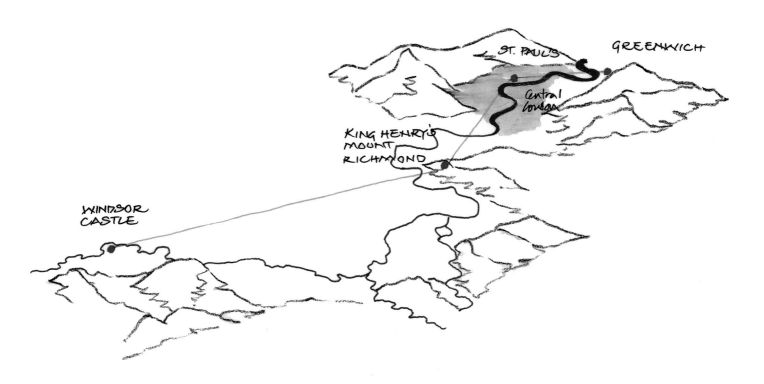

The high points along the Thames give vistas that connect Windsor Castle with Greenwich via Richmond Hill and St Paul's Cathedral.

it makes sense to the people who live and work there. The strategy was based on three years of daily observation of the river landscape; interviews with over 180 local interest groups and 50 official bodies; and extensive public consultation. It charted the historic, natural and recreation landscapes, crossing borough boundaries and legal jurisdictions to agree policies and projects for the next hundred years – the time it takes for an oak to reach maturity and for planning ambitions, which may seem impossible in the short term, to become realistic. Most importantly the strategy was written and illustrated in a way that made it possible for lay people to use.

Since it was published in 1994, the strategy has taken on a life of its own. All four local authorities and central government have supported and funded it and employed coordinators to continue to bring everyone together to decide on priorities for this part of London through its landscape. The current coordinator, Jason Debney, has managed to galvanize enormous enthusiasm for the component projects and continues to expand the bodies that fund and support the strategy. When presented as something that makes instinctive and emotional sense, landscape is a powerful tool that allows people not only to understand their surroundings, but also to feel as though it belongs to them and that they can have an effective voice in deciding how it changes.

Across the Atlantic in Pennsylvania, I have been working for the last five years with Longwood Gardens and the DuPont Foundation on a project to design a new entrance space to the gardens' vast sequence of glasshouses. Longwood covers over 405 hectares (1,000 acres) and is one of the premier gardens in the United States. Director Paul Redman is in the process of reviewing their long-term strategy and mission statement, and I proposed that, as well as creating fluidity and simplicity of movement, the new arrival space could demonstrate imaginative conservation of water and natural resources.

Longwood has nearly a million visitors a year and a rare ability to set standards of best practice over the whole continent. The gardens not only needed a dramatic outside space to complement the hectares of glass, but also a resolution to the significant level changes and the all-important first stop – lavatory restrooms. My proposal was therefore to mould the land into a sinuous form that would sweep south to the main gardens and entrance, tucking the new building into the land.

Working with the English architect Alex Michaelis, local Philadelphia landscape architects Wells Appel, and US building architects FMG, we designed a building that completely integrates into the topography. A curving spine of glass curls through the landform, creating a 185 metre (607 feet) long corridor of light with top-lit domed washrooms opening off the spine. The loos are based on the design of the harem in the Topkapi Palace in Istanbul. The domed ceilings work well structurally with the insulating

A glass-roofed corridor curves under the new landform at Longwood giving access to the underground lavatory restrooms. The corridor is lined with over 370 square metres (4,000 square feet) of ferns and orchids that provide as much oxygen as ninety trees. It is the largest green wall in North America.

soil above them and the shafts of sunlight from high above, bring a magical quality into the functional spaces. The corridor itself is 5 metres (16 feet) beneath the surface and the soft light on the walls is perfect for growing ferns and orchids. With the horticultural expertise of Longwood, we have created the largest green wall in North America, linking to the gardens' rainwater and grey-water harvesting systems. From the conservatory, visitors enter a watery world of lush vegetation, curving down a green tunnel to a raised circular pool with continuous views up to the sky and forest trees above.

The project has tried to create a place that is at once functional and beautiful, playful and educational. Our aim has been to show how simple, traditional techniques of insulating buildings underground and weaving them into landscape can create great spaces simultaneously inside and outside. This really is land and architecture; and the water closets celebrate water and plants in a visible loop.

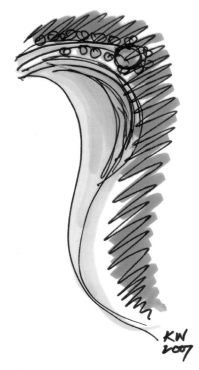

LEFT On the northern side of the spine the lavatory domes are visible and connect to the garden service area.

BELOW The landform curves southwards to the formal gardens, covering and insulating the lavatory complex, and visually links with the native woodland beyond.

SOIL

'Soil' is a lovely rich word that conjures up dark crumbling earth full of micro-organisms and worms. 'Turf' is almost as evocative – soft, green and supple. The American equivalents of 'dirt' and 'sod' somehow do not convey the same respect. That modest layer of fertile earth, teeming with microscopic life, is ultimately what makes life in the tiny bands of atmosphere and topsoil on the crust of the planet possible.

Cultivating the earth gives us agriculture, horticulture and domestic landscape. Deep within that process is an ideal of existence that recurs in civilization after civilization. Virgil is probably the most powerful maker of that image, describing a perfect harmony of innocent man tending the land and evoking the poetic shepherds of Hellenic Arcadia. The Italian Renaissance drew deeply on the Augustan poets and created a particular kind of suburban villa that allowed escape from the city to pure air, pure thought and physical activity.

LEFT The seventeenth-century *limonaia* still houses the lemon trees through the winter in a pattern of horticultural expertise that has not changed in over four hundred years.

BELOW Villa La Pietra from the garden. The Renaissance villa and its valley above Florence have now been restored by New York University.

Villa La Pietra is set in the foothills above Florence, 1.75 kilometres (1 mile) from the city gates along the ancient road to Bologna. It was initially built as the rural retreat of the Sassetti banking family in the fifteenth century. Acquired by Piero di Nicolo Capponi in 1545 and expanded by Scipione Capponi in the seventeenth century, the villa became a classic example of an elegant country house set on a ridge overlooking the Duomo and the centre of Florence. It was flanked by walled gardens and was highly productive in olives, grapes and vegetables as well as sophisticated luxuries such as flower and lemon extracts. The villa was simultaneously a place of food and poetry. Decamping to the hills to escape the summer heat was part of the goal, but there was something more profound. It was felt that the city was a place of noise, corruption and commerce

where it was hard to think. Involvement with the land and plants, and the sheer physical exercise of digging and pruning, cleared the head for poetry and philosophy. It was a place for *otium* – peace and leisure to contemplate – as opposed to the *negotium* of the town.

In 1907 Harold Acton's mother bought Villa La Pietra and, with her husband Arthur, set about restoring the house, garden and valley to their notion of a Renaissance ideal. Together with a Florence coterie of expatriate Anglo-Americans, they had enormous influence on garden design and early twentieth-century country house culture. Vita Sackville-West came to stay while she was creating the garden at Sissinghurst, as did Lawrence Johnston, the owner of Hidcote.

When he died in 1994, Harold Acton left the estate to New York University, which has been painstakingly restoring the villa and gardens ever since. Harold particularly liked the idea of young students enjoying Florentine art and gardens and chose a university with a sufficiently deep pocket and dedication to the place to bring the villa and gardens back to health.

The restoration of the garden posed some interesting questions. Apart from half of Scipione's walled garden, most of the Renaissance archaeology had been destroyed by the construction of a romantic 'English Garden' by the Incontri family in the nineteenth century. Arthur and Hortense Acton, Harold's parents, spent decades unpicking the nineteenth-century changes and creating a very individual interpretation of a formal Renaissance garden that would display their growing collection of garden statuary. The Acton garden reached its peak in the 1930s before the Second World War. The place was well documented by photographs and, though by 1994 many of the structural plants had died out, enough stumps and bumps remained to enable an accurate restoration. The significance of the Acton garden and the surviving evidence of its layout made the decision to restore to the 1930s peak relatively uncontroversial.

What was more troubling was the charm of the near derelict garden, with its collapsing pavilions and toppling statues. How were we to restore the garden without completely destroying the magic and poetry of the place? New York University was very understanding about the proposal to take the work gradually. Unconventionally we felled the failing trees and hedges first, replanting the precise lines of yew and cypress architectural

The restoration of the garden has taken fifteen years, starting with replanting the trees and hedges and gradually moving on to the crumbling stone. We have tried to keep the wistful magic of the place through the rather brutal process.

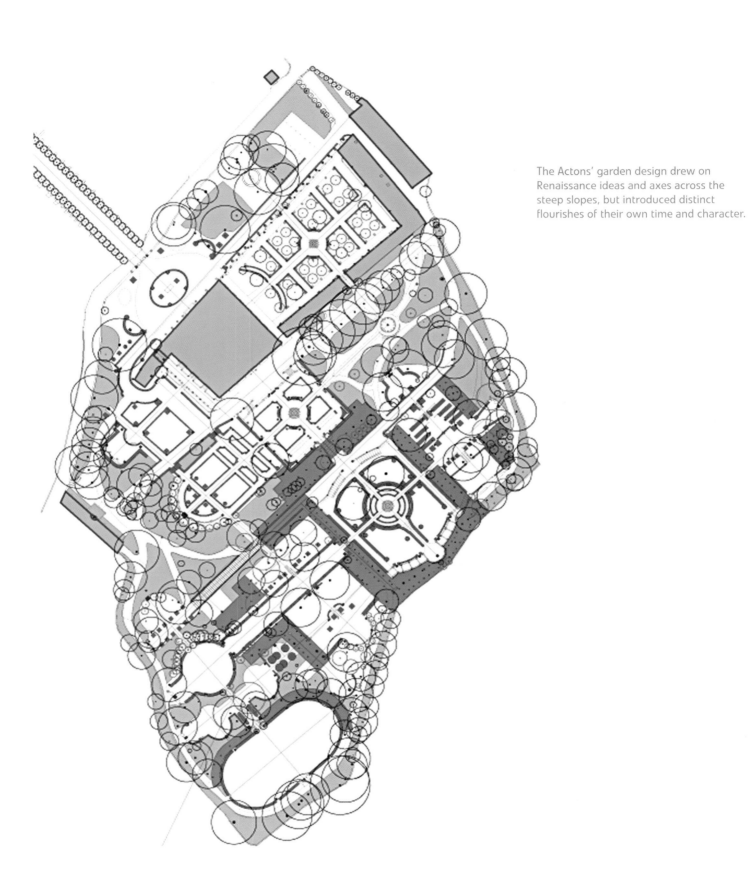

The Actons' garden design drew on
Renaissance ideas and axes across the
steep slopes, but introduced distinct
flourishes of their own time and character.

structure before tackling the crumbling walls, fountains and buildings. Somehow the memories of the place managed to take refuge in the stone while the green architecture reassembled itself. Fifteen years later the garden is really coming back into its own, with the patterns of light and shade falling sharply on crisp topiary, while mellow stone, frogs and glow worms soften the ridge-top garden.

The head gardener, Nick Dakin-Elliot, has been key to the process, bringing solid expertise on everything from drainage and foundations to pruning and propagation. His constant presence, guidance of the gardening team and patience with local legislation have made the restoration possible. An early triumph was the replanting of Scipione's walled vegetable garden and the restoration of the major collection of lemon trees in eighteenth-century pots. Villa La Pietra is now as productive as it was in the Renaissance.

Soil conservation and productivity have been the basis of the project. The estate straddles two sides of a 23 hectare (57 acre) valley and the main Renaissance villa is supported by four further villas on the perimeter of the property. These have adapted well to teaching and dormitory facilities for the students. The central valley has now been replanted with olive groves and an ambitious plan for rainwater collection and grey-water recycling is under consideration. Villa La Pietra shows the resilience of an age-old concept of living sustainably on the land, which can survive through changing cultures and landownership; from a fifteenth-century Medici banker, to a sixteenth-century cardinal, to a twentieth-century English art dealer and a twenty-first century American university. The essence and philosophy of the place have remained constant.

The walled vegetable garden survives from the time of Scipione Capponi and continues to feed the villa. Fiesole can be seen in the distance.

The long cross vista terminates in the outdoor theatre, one of the early introductions to the garden by the Actons.

The theatre has been a place of great entertainment over the years. Margot Fonteyn, Brigitte Bardot and more recently Judi Dench and Antony Sher have all performed in the space. The box balls were planted to conceal the limelights.

THE APOTHECARIES' GARDEN
MOSCOW

The Apothecaries' Garden in Moscow shows a similar resilience and ability to adapt while still keeping its core mission and identity. In 1706 Peter the Great founded the garden as a place to raise and study medicinal plants. He was fascinated by science and keen to bring the latest thoughts and technologies to Russia. Legend has it that Peter himself planted three of the original garden conifers with his own hands. The ancient Siberian larch, which still survives in the garden, is thought to be one of these.

The garden originally belonged to the Moscow Hospital and was then handed on to the Medical Academy. The first director of the garden, appointed in 1735, was both a doctor of medicine and a prominent botanist. By 1804 the Medical Academy had moved to the new capital, St Petersburg, and the garden was bought by Moscow University in the following year. It is interesting to follow the evolution of medical and botanical science, as well as the changing tastes in layout and design, that the history of the garden reflects.

The eighteenth-century orthogonal compartments of ordered physic plants, beside a rectangular reservoir to store rainwater, gradually softened into serpentine paths, lawns, free-standing trees and a picturesque lake. By the time of Catherine the Great, the 'English taste' had reached Russia and the garden began to resemble more of an urban park than an ordered physic garden. The emphasis and design of the garden altered with changing priorities in science, medicine, education and recreation over the centuries, but the focus on plants and their display for teaching, curiosity and delight remained. During the nineteenth century the garden became fully romantic and Chekhovian, but Soviet re-emphasis on science returned order beds and experimental plantings for analysis of food and crop varieties.

In the first hundred years the plant collection rapidly expanded from medicinal to wider botanical and taxonomic curiosity. By 1808 director Hoffmann had recorded over 3,500 species in the garden. Growing plants in the extremes of Moscow heat and cold is not easy – glasshouses are essential – but political upheaval proved almost as challenging as the climate. During the 1812 Napoleonic occupation of Moscow most of the greenhouses were destroyed, along with many plants and part of the library and herbarium. The garden recovered but had to raise funds by selling off land, so reducing the area from 9 to 7.2 hectares (22 to 18 acres). Despite the Revolution, the Second World

The redesigned entrance to the Apothecaries' Garden in Moscow. The axial canal reflects the old glasshouse and is framed by Siberian birches and pines.

War and Moscow University's acquisition of a much larger site to the south west, the Apothecaries' Garden somehow managed to survive as a much-loved space in the centre of a rapidly developing city.

The latest rescue of the garden is largely thanks to the dedicated cooperation of the Moscow botanist Alexei Reteyum and landscape architect Artyom Parshin, with the architect developers Sergei and Georgi Gevorkyan. Together they have brought the garden back to life, developing cafés, restaurants and offices along the street edges and restoring the crumbling glasshouses and failing collections. They invited me to draw up

a masterplan for the garden in 1997. Moscow was then a very different city, just emerging into a modern economy and facing conflicting pressures.

Working with the garden team and the architectural historian Dmitry Schvidkovsky, we agreed to restore as much of the historic garden as possible. The Chekhovian paths, lake and groves have all been saved and the original lime avenues that frame the garden are now in good health. The glasshouses have been expanded, incorporating the earlier façades, and the library has been rescued. Two new areas were incorporated as part of the masterplan: an entrance to draw people in from the south-

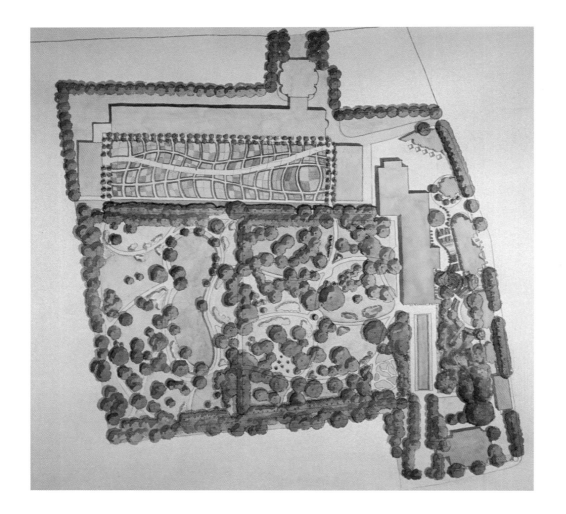

The Apothecaries' Garden survives as one of the significant open spaces in the centre of Moscow. It is now surrounded by major buildings (RIGHT), but the frame of lime avenues still encloses the garden (CENTRE) and the new plan incorporates the eighteenth- and nineteenth-century layers with functional contemporary spaces that have helped to revive and reinvigorate the gardens (LEFT).

west corner and a new interpretation of order beds on a former works yard in the north east. The new entrance combines a long reflecting pool leading to the glasshouses with groups of Russian birches and pines on either side. For the works yard I proposed a grid of rectangular order beds, warped in three dimensions to accommodate changes in drainage and aspect. The works yard plans have not yet been implemented. The Russians have a deep passion for gardening, especially for fruit and vegetables, and the idea is to provide a combination of demonstration and experimental plots in a fresh and sculptural layout that still remembers the early eighteenth-century physic garden.

OXFORD BOTANIC GARDEN
OXFORD

Oxford Botanic Garden charts a less turbulent but in some ways parallel history. It was founded by Sir Henry Danvers in the seventeenth century as a physic garden for 'the glorification of God and for the furtherance of learning'. The garden is set within high stone walls beside the River Cherwell and was from the start used to research the scientific and medicinal values of plants. Sir Isaac Bayley Balfour laid out rectangular botanical family borders to his adaptation of the Bentham and Hooker system of classifying plants. In the last decade plant classification has moved on significantly. The Botanic Garden has rearranged the family beds to represent the latest developments, using DNA to create an evolutionary tree for flowering plants.

After the Second World War the Botanic Garden was offered an area of Christ Church allotments beyond the walls of the seventeenth-century garden. Initially the area was developed as a display of ornamental herbaceous plants and flowering shrubs. In 2004, following our plans for the university's Harcourt Arboretum, I was asked by the Botanic Garden to make proposals to rejuvenate the area. Having worked on botanic gardens in Chile and Moscow and considered the future of the Royal Botanic Gardens at Kew as part of the Thames Landscape Strategy, my head was buzzing with possibilities.

The Oxford Botanic Garden is small and perfectly formed. The position between Magdalen, Merton and Christ Church colleges beside the Cherwell is stunning. Its history as the oldest botanic garden in England and the legacy of scientific thought and

The Oxford Botanic Garden is bounded by the River Cherwell and makes an ideal place to demonstrate water plants purifying and recirculating clean water.

The new plan has been to create
an area of fruit and vegetables
beyond the seventeenth-century
walls, showing how plants can be
grown successfully in an urban
environment to produce food and
clean air and water.

The Botanic Garden's position in the centre of Oxford brings in large numbers of visitors as well as students and groups of schoolchildren.

educational expertise are impressive. Most of all the inner-city location by Magdalen Bridge makes the garden an easy and attractive destination for thousands of visitors a year. It reaches students, schoolchildren, Oxford residents and tourists. We discussed which message the Botanic Garden would most like to communicate to its broad audience. As a counterpoint to the scientific beds within the walls and given the earlier history of the Christ Church land as allotments, I suggested that the ultramures area could become an elegant demonstration of inner-urban sustainability – a place to show how to grow fruit and vegetables in a city and to collect and purify water using plants.

Together with the university team of Louise Allen and Piers Newth, we developed a plan to combine vegetable plots, fruit trees, and ornamental and water plants on a logical grid that related to the beds within the walls and the axial arrangement on the archway tower to Magdalen. To make the most of the space, the new layout is fractured to pick up a dramatic vista to Merton tower, creating a diagonal axis that breaks the linear pattern and helps to bring in views to the river and the centre of Oxford. The vegetables are now harvested and donated to local charities through an organization called the Oxford Food Bank.

At the same time we have been talking to the Environment Agency about making a connection to the River Cherwell and demonstrating how reed beds and filtration through water plants can cleanse water naturally. We have also been working with the sculptor Keith Wilson on initial proposals to turn the rather tired rose garden, owned by Magdalen College at the front of the Botanic Garden, into a new design demonstrating water collection and purification techniques, though this has not yet gone forward.

The south-facing wall and garden area beyond the historic order beds are ideal for growing food.

The vegetables grown in the garden are distributed to local charities through the Oxford Food Bank.

The Chelsea Barracks project has offered some interesting parallels in decisions about priorities for land within the city. The site covers 5.2 hectares (12.8 acres) in south-west London and is being redeveloped at a turning point in our attitude to cities and the environment. The combination of climate change, financial upheaval and political transition has focused attention on how to make settlements succeed in the future. The relationship between open spaces and buildings will be a key to the way forward. The scale, location and level of investment and long-term management in this site make it possible to create a way of living that can set an exemplary pattern.

Interestingly the decision was taken to plan the development around the spaces rather than the buildings. A detailed planning application for the landscape and public realm has been approved while the various building envelopes are limited to outline parameters. The individual architects for each part of the plan will be selected shortly, but the masterplan itself combined architects and landscape architects, drawing together the competition-winning practices of Dixon Jones, Michael Squire and Partners and Kim Wilkie Associates to produce a joint vision.

The main aim of the strategy was to reopen the site to the patterns of movement and spaces in the surrounding city. The guiding principle was to make the place as permeable as possible and to encourage the public to walk throughout the area. Streets, squares, shops, cafés and sports, cultural and health facilities should make the development feel like a regular part of the urban realm. There will be a typical range of public, semi-private and private spaces. Garrison Square will form the physical and

The redevelopment of the Chelsea Barracks site in London comes at a turning point in our attitude to cities and the environment. The landscape concept is to create a sequence of squares and gardens that are inspired by the stewardship of soil, air and water.

BELOW The masterplan is laid out as a series of London squares that integrate with the surrounding urban pattern and encourage people to walk through and use the spaces.

RIGHT The old Garrison Chapel survives at the centre of the site and is planned to become a focus for art, music and a weekly farmers' market linked to the adjacent productive garden.

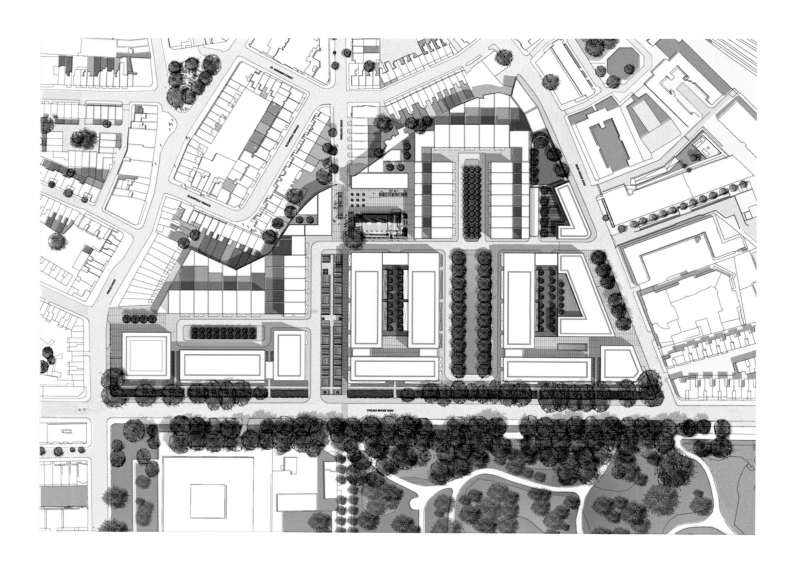

social centre of the development and the refurbished chapel will take on a focal role as a place for music, art, display and gatherings. The Orange Square farmers' market will also be invited to use the square on Saturdays.

The landscape concept is to create a variety of gardens, squares and courts that are inspired by the stewardship of soil, water and air. As well as offering play and recreation, the open spaces will capture rainwater, filter air, compost waste, nourish wildlife and even grow food. The combination of deep, well-watered soils on the leafy suburban edge of London historically made Chelsea a prime place for growing fruit and vegetables to feed the capital. The healthy position upstream and upwind of central London, together with speedy connections along the river, turned the area into a popular place to live for people like Sir Thomas More (resident at Beaufort House 1520–35) and a prime location for the Royal Hospital (founded by Charles II in 1681). The fashionable suburban idyll was protected and perpetuated by the residential squares developed by

We are working with Sarah Raven to create an intensely productive garden through the main square of the new development. The garden will be 100 metres (328 feet) long and be run by professional gardeners with the fruit, salads and vegetables being served in a new restaurant and sold in Garrison Square.

the Grosvenor and Cadogan Estates in the eighteenth and nineteenth centuries.

London squares create an excellent template for productive and sustainable open spaces. While they provide a familiar and comfortable format of green rectangles lined by trees and protected by railings, squares are extraordinarily adaptable in terms of use and planting. At the centrepiece of the axial entrance to the new neighbourhood there will be a 100 metre (328 foot) long productive garden. It will make a clear statement about the character and philosophy of the development as an immaculately tended herb, fruit and vegetable garden leading up to the central square, with its farmers' market and destination restaurant. There will be two full-time expert vegetable gardeners working in the open beds and glasshouses.

The garden will be lush and sculptural in the way that the gardens of vegetables at the Château de Villandry in the Loire manage to look as polished as any parterre. Yet at the same time, the garden will be vigorously managed to grow vegetables, herbs and salads that will be sold in the restaurant and market, demonstrating that it is both practical and beautiful to grow perishable food in the centre of cities. I have been working with Sarah Raven to design a practical rotation of salads and vegetables to succeed commercially as well as look attractive throughout the year. Polished ochre and red masonry will create a grid of 6 metre (20 foot) square raised planters, underlit with bright colours. A central pedestrian path will be lined by narrow lit rills of fast-moving water, circulating the rainwater harvested from the new neighbourhood. Sculptural stainless-steel Archimedes screws will raise the water from the rills to irrigate the beds. A pair of contemporary glasshouses will be built at the centre of the garden in which to grow seedlings for the productive beds. Specially designed bronze railings will enclose the perimeter of the garden, acting as a frame for plants such as sweet peas and runner beans. Basal heat from the mechanical and engineering plant beneath the garden will keep plants growing vigorously throughout the winter.

This is a chance to show that even in the richest international neighbourhoods, growing food and harvesting natural resources can be an integral and welcomed part of design. Urban farming is not just for Detroit wastelands or Havana deprivation; it can form a sensible and acceptable part of every development.

Victoria and Albert Museum, London

LIFE

The word 'picturesque' usually makes me nervous. It has a smell of formaldehyde. Life and movement are the blood of landscape and they cannot be reduced to a static picture. The eighteenth-century concept of the 'animated prospect' came much closer to an understanding of how we relate to land. The activity that we watch and share in a place turns scenery into landscape. And the lives that we simultaneously remember and imagine into that landscape, give it depth and resonance.

WILDLIFE

The European landscape has been settled for so many millennia that wildlife and humans have rather come to rely on one another. We know that we need wildlife. There is, for example, a panic of fragile impotence when we realize what would happen to the pollination of our food plants if bees were wiped out by the varroa mite. But wildlife also needs us. Ancient woodlands are a great example. The woods were a carefully and intensely managed resource that kept a balance of light and renewal in their structure and in turn provided a very rich habitat for vegetation, insects and birds. Ash coppice in particular is a precious habitat that relies on a rotation of cutting. Since the Second World War forestry management in the United Kingdom has struggled economically and much coppice woodland has been abandoned. Four-hundred-year-old ash coppices are now falling over for lack of management and centuries of established habitat are being lost.

The city of Winchester sits comfortably in its downland landscape. The water meadows have been protected and the cathedral remains the dominant building in the town. The Hampshire Wildlife Trust has restored the meadows at Winnall Moors on the northern edge of Winchester (LEFT) and the wildflowers and bird populations have flourished.

Rachel Carson's *Silent Spring* of 1962 helped to inform a mounting popular outrage at the destruction of habitats by industrial farming and urban expansion. In the fury it is sometimes forgotten what an important role farmers can play in conserving the habitats that survive. The wet meadows around Winchester are a very good example. Of all the cities in England, Winchester has managed to sit particularly comfortably in its landscape. The settlement shelters in a valley bowl where the waters of the River Itchen collect. The web of streams and channels and their inherent defences helped Alfred the Great to choose the town as his capital. Marshy Winchester was reputedly the last place in Britain where you could catch malaria.

The Norman shift to London allowed Winchester to sleep on as a provincial city. Today you can still walk from the Iron Age fort in the open downland, across the medieval

The medieval wet meadows at Winchester College are a rare habitat for birds, wildflowers and spawning salmon. Photographs and paintings from between the wars show the meadows as open and well grazed (BELOW). Following the economic crisis in livestock farming, grazing ceased and the meadows quickly became covered in sycamore, scrub and Japanese Knotweed (OPPOSITE), greatly reducing the wildlife value of the land. Winchester College will now be removing the invasive species and reintroducing grazing to the meadows.

water meadows, through the King's Gate in the city walls and the Priory Gate to the Cathedral Close and reach the Buttercross in the very centre of the city without passing a petrol station, a Tesco or a B&Q. What is more, when you look back out from the Buttercross, you can still see the open hillsides that surround the city and when you approach from a distance the towers of the cathedral, the guildhall, the prison and Winchester College chapel stand out as the principal buildings. Tess of the d'Urberville's hanging tower is the first glimpse of the city from miles away. Town and countryside remain united.

Landownership as well as topography and hydrology have helped this union to survive. The south-eastern quadrant of the city is largely owned by the cathedral and Winchester College, and between them they have combined to conserve the medieval buildings and wet landscape that stretches out to the chalk downland and the Iron Age fort. Interestingly the soggy land was carefully managed as state-of-the-art medieval farming. The meadows were criss-crossed with ditches, channels and sluices that enabled the farmers to flood and drain the land to capture

Winchester is an excellent example of a city that has stayed closely connected to its landscape. Many of the buildings are made of the local flint stone; the intimate medieval streets, courtyards and closes are good places for modern life. The views and paths between the surrounding hills and the city centre have survived for over a thousand years.

warmth and fertility and gain precious weeks of early spring grass growth to fatten their sheep and cows. Technologically the water meadows were very precise and highly advanced.

Although the intensive management of the water waned with the decline of agriculture, the meadows continued to be grazed until the 1970s. The plight of the British dairy industry then led to the removal of herds across the country and the abandonment of wet meadows from Surrey to Suffolk. Within a decade the abandoned land had sprouted trees and a decade later meadows that had been tended and open for over a thousand years had become thickets of poplar, sycamore, Japanese knotweed and brambles. The change to the landscape was fundamental, but because the transformation happened gradually, year by year, it largely went unnoticed. Stubble developed slowly into a full beard and people forgot that the land had ever been close shaven. Trees are seen as intrinsically good and any proposal to chop them down and revert to grazing and management as unnatural and brutal. Rachel Carson's army has taken on a moral as well as a political and philosophical intensity.

Natural England, the government body responsible for the natural environment, has valiantly tried to explain the enormous wildlife significance of these wet meadows. The interaction between wildflowers, insects, birds, small mammals and fish that the gentle habitat supports is generous and complex. But the relationship between humans and wildlife has increasingly been oversimplified by a predominantly urban population into 'wild good, human bad'. An urban reaction has developed to assume that if you were just to remove humans from the picture, everything would be fine and nature could take care of herself. Over centuries this might be true, but in the short term a great deal of our most treasured wildlife would be in trouble.

When we proposed the felling of many of the trees on the Winchester wet meadows and the reintroduction of cattle as part of the masterplan for the College, there was growling protest from local residents. The College kept its nerve and explained the history and the science of the landscape to everyone who was interested. After a series of public meetings the consensus shifted from objection to general, and often enthusiastic, support. The adjacent grazed St Cross meadows to the south-west showed how beautiful and rich in wildlife the ancient landscape could be. And to the north-east, the restoration of Winnall Moors by the

Hampshire Wildlife Trust demonstrated how rapidly meadows of wildflowers could be recovered. There are still decades of discussion to be had about how cattle and salmon can coexist and how much stream banks can be trampled, but at least the understanding of the complex interconnections within the landscape has improved. Local people have become more connected with their environment, the delicate wildlife habitats will be saved, and the views between the cathedral and the Iron Age fort will be reopened.

Conservation of healthy landscape has to look forward. The economics of land management and the demands for food, recreation and carbon sequestration all press on the priorities and perceptions of landscape — Alexander Pope's 'use' as well as his 'genius'. Managing land well does not necessarily mean farming it in a historic way or even to a historic appearance; just learning good lessons from the past that might be applicable in the future.

SHAWFORD WET MEADOWS
HAMPSHIRE

Downstream from Winchester at Shawford, the approach was very different. Between two arms of the river, 25 hectares (60 acres) of old meadow had been laser levelled in the late twentieth century to construct a helipad and polo pitch. Both were made redundant by a change in ownership. The land is attached to a fine Carolean house and the new owners asked me to design gardens to complement the house and create a watery landscape to fit the wider environment.

Changes in layout and landownership over the centuries had erased the archaeology and relevance of earlier gardens and the sprawl of island beds and pampas grass into the wilder landscape had muddled the setting. It was time for a new design that would draw the formal gardens in around the house and release the remaining landscape back to the river. Flooding, deer and badgers urged protection for the cultivated areas, especially as a large part of the new gardens were to be laid out as vegetable parterres. The language of seventeenth-century design is strong and architectural. I was able to make an earth rampart that would wrap around the garden, hiding a deer fence in a sunken ditch beyond and creating a raised walkway to gaze over the landscape. A corner bastion provides a lookout for Anthony Gormley's *Watcher*.

The landscape at Shawford Park is a new interpretation of a wet meadow. Curving channels have been carved down to the water table to create warm, shallow rills of alkaline water, which is the perfect habitat for the southern damselfly. Wildlife habitats can be sculptural as well as functional. The photograph shows the hay cut, ready for collection and grazing.

The curving channels have been designed to run from an old stew pond down to the River Itchen. In the twentienth century the stew pond had been covered by a car park and the meadows levelled for a helipad and polo pitch. We removed those developments and created a water landscape, separated from the formal gardens by ramparts and bastions. From the rampart you can look over the new quilted landform (FAR RIGHT) with mist rising from the water rills.

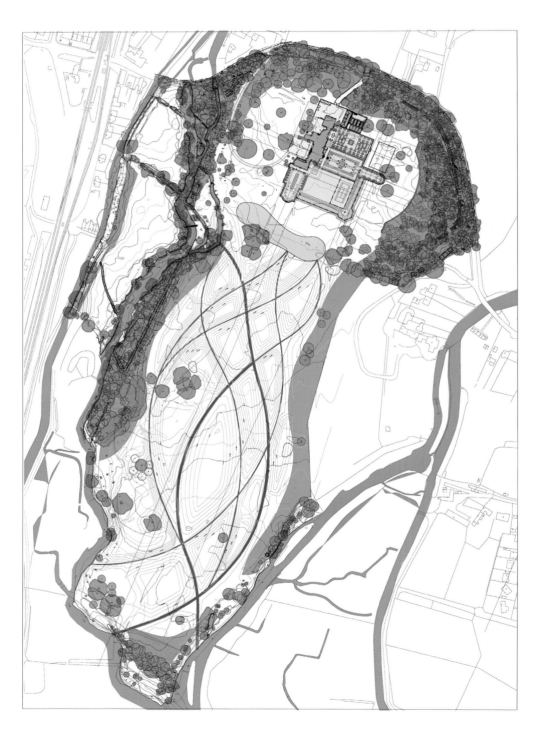

Beyond the rampart, the helipad and polo pitch have now been ripped out and the land parted down to the water table. The old stew or fish pond has been reopened as a lake and curving channels of water course through the landscape collecting spring water to feed the river. Between the channels the earth has been mounded to create a sinuous quilted landscape of sheep-grazed wildflowers. On autumn evenings the river mist rises eerily from the channels emphasizing the quilted form. Winter frost turns the meadows into a white sculpture.

This is a completely new landform. It is neither a recreation of a water meadow nor the conjectural reconstruction of the seventeenth-century landscape. Understanding the traditions of allowing the water to flow through the land and studying the native plants that used to flourish in the area helped to inform and inspire the design. Most particularly the distress of the endangered southern damselfly was key to making the space. This native turquoise dragonfly has almost gone extinct as meadows have been abandoned and become covered by trees

and shrubs. It needs warm, shallow, flowing alkaline water in full sun to feed and breed. The weaving open water we created is exactly the habitat it needs. Both the damselfly and the otters had moved in before we had finished, blithely relaxed about the diggers and the dumpers.

Cohabitation with historic sites and fragile wildlife need not confine us to a static pattern of conservation and land management. It is critical to understand what is significant and vulnerable, but that can be a great source of inspiration for new design and fresh management, finely detailed to the place and its special peculiarities. With the right knowledge and sensitivity, you can leap into new territories with humour and relevance. Respect for the past and concern for wildlife can be a real stimulus for fresh ideas.

In winter frost picks out the shapes and curves and a Gormley *Watcher* observes from the new bastion in the corner of the rampart.

On another wet meadow site, in Suffolk, seventeenth-century fish ponds had silted up and become covered by alder, while the rest of the valley had been planted with tight grids of poplars. The Blithe Valley is a gentle landform with a narrow river, almost a stream, meandering down its centre. Although the valley is understated, it has some dramatic buildings on its banks. The Blithe flows past the old parish churches of Huntingfield and Walpole, which mark the western and eastern sides of the valley bowl. Huntingfield and Heveningham Halls stand to the north and south of the river. The whole landscape of trees, buildings and water had been designed to work together across the open, grazed meadows at their centre. When the meadows became filled with trees, none of the historic views and landscape relationships could be seen.

Heveningham Hall is one of those perfect eighteenth-century country houses that had the best designers of the day. Sir Robert Taylor built the hall; James Wyatt made the interiors; and Lancelot Brown designed the landscape. Unfortunately Brown died the year after the design and his plans were never implemented, but he left behind an exquisite 3 metre (10 foot) long watercoloured drawing that is so accurate that it can be superimposed on a contemporary digital topographic survey. You can even pick out the species of the proposed trees from the delicate profiles he painted. Brown's design was simple but inspired. He suggested framing the valley crest with thick, undulating woodland to give protection and definition to the estate. Parkland was to flow down

Heveningham Hall is a perfect eighteenth-century English country house, designed by the top architect, decorator and landscape architect of the day.

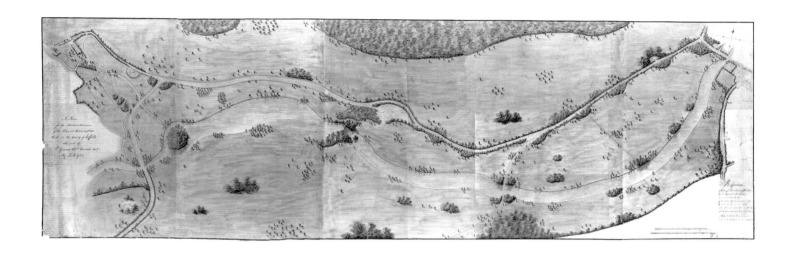

from the hall and over the river, uniting both sides of the valley. The little river was to be left undisturbed, but the fish ponds beside it were to be expanded into a broad, long lake. The lake was to have the appearance of a generous river lazily curving through the landscape. The expanse of water, reflecting the sky, was designed to give the valley a scale and grandeur to complement Taylor's new mansion.

Brown's plans managed to combine simple bold gestures with finely detailed vistas. The positioning of trees and parkland clumps cleverly directed the eye away from the centre of the valley, where the view is at its shortest and the lake has to change level as the valley descends towards Walpole. It also helped to direct symmetrical pairs of views to east and west. At opposite ends of the valley, the tower of Huntingfield church and the spire of Walpole church are framed by clumps of trees. Then, less obliquely, the vista to Huntingfield Hall was matched by a corresponding vista to an old farmhouse. Huntingfield Hall was refaced as a gothick folly and Brown designed a classical façade for the farmhouse to resemble a Greek temple.

Two centuries later, Heveningham had fallen on hard times. Fires, inheritance tax and sudden death had left the place empty with most of the land sold. After languishing on the market for several years, the house was bought in 1995 by a young family who set about restoring the landscape and the hall and gradually piecing together the original landownership.

Lancelot Brown's landscape plan (TOP LEFT) was so accurate that it could be implemented two centuries after it was drawn and the lake and parkland (BELOW) have been created exactly as he drew it. The landscape was skilfully designed to frame key views, such as the vista across the valley to the refaced Huntingfield Hall (BELOW LEFT).

Now, sixteen years later, the estate has grown from under 200 hectares (500 acres) to over 1,600 hectares (4,000 acres). Nearly 2 kilometres (1.3 miles) of lakes have been dug that in places are up to 60 metres (66 yards) wide. A 40 metre (44 yard) stone bridge has been built across the water, as Brown proposed. Nearly 160 hectares (400 acres) of grazed meadow and parkland have been created and 240 hectares (600 acres) of broadleaved native woodland planted.

The project was initially something of a conundrum for English Heritage. Although the hall is listed as Grade I and the faithful creation of a Brownian landscape surrounding the house was theoretically a good idea, the proposals could not be described as a historic restoration. The Brownian landscape had only ever existed on plan and the implementation of his designs 200 years

later would technically be a new insertion into a historic landscape. Further headaches arose with the silted fish pond, which had become an alder carr of nature conservation interest. It took eighteen months of research, consultation and negotiation to agree the masterplan with all the various authorities and it will probably take another 100 years before the landscape comes to maturity. But the exciting thing has been that the vision of an entire estate, designed seven years before the French Revolution, still remains relevant today. The mosaic of habitats created by the water, parkland, woodland and hedgerows is wonderfully rich in wildlife. It has transformed the bird, insect and mammal life of this corner of Suffolk by converting miles of arable land into many different, interrelated habitats that combine native woodland edges with grazed wildflower pasture; reedy river banks with wet meadow; hedgerows with ditches; and bat-filled old buildings with stretches of insect-rich open water. The place is beautiful but it is also alive.

As a social as well as landscape focus, Heveningham has also been rejuvenated. An annual fair is now held at the hall and raises over £30,000 each year to be split between the five parishes that ring the estate. Quite apart from the funds raised and the fun had, the weekly meetings leading up to the fair each year bring the community together in a powerful and voluble way. The hall is not just the physical and architectural centre of the landscape. It has become a symbol of the local community as well.

The combination of grazed pasture, wet meadow, meandering river, open water and managed woodland create interconnected habitats that make Heveningham a haven for wildlife and a focal centre to the landscape.

PEOPLE

Humans are as much a part of the landscape as wildlife. Designing spaces for busy human activity is as enjoyable and challenging as creating rich wildlife habitats. Part of the function of the public realm is to make places for spontaneous human contact in a rushing city. The public realm should be truly democratic space where everyone feels both safe and welcome. It stretches beyond streets and parks to railway stations, churches and museums. These places have many roles and the same spot can change with time of day, season or event. A space may need to switch between relaxed deckchairs, marathons and political demonstrations, as at Hyde Park or the Victoria Embankment. Such spaces need not always be comfortable; they can sometimes inspire awe. Las Colinas Square in Dallas is a harsh expanse of baking stone with a diagonal slash of water and bronze mustangs across the middle. It is a hostile spot, but hugely popular in the air-conditioned city for giving a sense of the land beneath its sealed complacency. Whatever their character or purpose, urban spaces are always about bringing people out of their private corners to interact with the wider world.

Spaces for solitude and contemplation are nevertheless important too, though they are often overlooked in justification by quantification. Political allocation of value usually relates to numbers satisfied, but the quality of life is hard to reduce to numbers. I have been struck by the public spaces that open up briefly on the foreshore of the Thames between tides. Beaches and walks along gravel spits allow people to walk alone peacefully beside the water and forget for a moment that they are in the middle of a huge metropolis. Urban sanity may depend on time to wander and ponder on your own.

Comfortable solitude in the city is as precious as gathering spaces. The foreshore that opens up at Chiswick Mall in London (LEFT) allows people to stroll along the gravel banks, surrounded by water while the tide is out. At the Victoria and Albert Museum, not far away (BELOW), visitors can paddle in the reflecting pond in the centre of the museum.

The Victoria and Albert Museum has one of the best collections of art and design in the world, with over four and a half million treasures. You can wander in it for days, constantly surprised by the variety of the collections, from iron cemetery crosses to the latest contemporary designs of glass. Although one of the pleasures of the place is to become lost in the labyrinth and be endlessly amazed by the eccentricity and beauty of human art and imagination, the museum is aiming to become more accessible and approachable.

The Future Plan for the V&A is succeeding in making the labyrinth easier to navigate and understand. The complex of buildings covers over 5 hectares (12.5 acres) in south-west London. At the centre of the site is a courtyard garden that brings light and a fulcrum of orientation into the heart of the museum. This courtyard used to be the main entrance when the museum was first laid out by Francis Fowke in 1852. At that

stage the entrance was designed as a grand Italianate façade, set back 100 metres (110 yards) from the Cromwell Road. As the museum grew and new galleries were built, the grand entrance was cut off from the road by a new southern wing designed by Aston Webb in 1899. This resulted in an intimately proportioned space (60 x 40 metres/66 x 44 yards) that sits beneath a super-confident façade that was designed to be viewed from a distance. In the past the style and scale of the architecture disconcerted some people and the courtyard garden has been through a few permutations. A garden of cherry trees was replaced by dense plantings of alders and incense cedars aimed to damp down the architecture. The combination of deep shade from the trees and dark film on the museum windows against ultraviolet light meant that many visitors passed by without even being aware of the courtyard. The Future Plan aimed to change all this and turn the garden into a pivotal space at the centre of the museum. A single donation from John Madejski made the project possible.

In 2005 the V&A held an international competition for a new courtyard garden. The competition came with a brief that simultaneously made complete sense and yet seemed impossible to achieve. The museum wanted a green and intimate garden where two people would feel relaxed and comfortable – so far so good; that would be flexible for displays, events, cafés and fairs – tricky; and that could instantly transform into a performance space for 2,000 and then turn back into a gentle garden again – a challenge. The space is small, the architecture is big and the uses gloriously unpredictable.

We managed to win the competition, proposing water as the solution. Rather than hide the façade behind mounding and trees, the idea was to open up and reveal the architecture. Digging down allows the former entrance once more to be approached up steps, giving the building back its feet and ankles. And creating an expanse of reflecting water bounces in light and doubles the sense of space. Most importantly for the use of the courtyard, the water is deceptively shallow and can be drained away to a tank in less than an hour, creating a large stone performance space. So the garden can indeed metamorphose from a tranquil oasis of grass and water into an intense gathering for 2,000 or more and then back again in the space of an afternoon.

The Victoria and Albert Museum courtyard garden with an elliptical reflecting pool that brings light and movement into the space. The pool can be drained in less than an hour to create a performance space for a couple of thousand people.

Constructing that space in less than six months was a whole further challenge. Extracting tonnes of spoil from an internal courtyard, through a museum stuffed with delicate treasures and people, is not easy. The first thought was to crane everything out over the roofs, but it quickly became apparent that temporarily reinforcing the roofs, in case a tonne load fell off the crane, was going to be more expensive than the rest of the project put together. In the end we opted for thirty wheelbarrows with thirty very fit Ukranians. In an age of computerized mechanization,

the power of human muscle should not be underestimated. We opened on time – just – on 5 July 2005.

The V&A has been wonderfully relaxed about letting people use the space. You are allowed to lie on the grass, paddle in the water and move the chairs around wherever you choose to sit. The result has been to create a truly flexible garden protected from noise and traffic with a warm microclimate right in the heart of Museumland. Visitors have not only increased in numbers but also diversified across age and cultures. Many

more young people and children now come to the museum, attracted by the garden. Some of them may not even visit the exhibits but, with the logic of the Jesuits, if you can persuade people to come in through the great doors as young children, the chances of them returning to explore as adults are greatly increased.

The V&A has also refurbished the gallery along the southern side as a space for sculpture, so the doors can now open and the dark film be peeled off the windows. In combination with the new restaurant on the north side, the whole courtyard zone becomes a welcoming fulcrum. At night it turns into yet another kind of space. I worked with the lighting designer Patrick Woodroffe to make the garden a dramatic place for

The V&A garden has a special microclimate that enables us to grow tender plants such as *Echium pininana* and *Geranium maderense*. Fountains echo the form of the planting and at night the space is used for special events. Glass planters glow like ice cubes and Patrick Woodroffe has lit the building to emphasize the depth and detail of the window reveals.

evening events. Rather than wash the walls with uplights, he introduced special Italian fixtures designed to illuminate the surrounds of each window, giving the building an extraordinary depth and life. I have also had a long fascination with glass and managed to design planters as cubes of glass that are lit from beneath, looking like lumps of glacial ice around the reflecting water.

The microclimate makes the garden a great place for plants. *Echium pininana*, *Salvia guaranitica*, *Geranium maderense* and *Agapanthus africanus* all thrive in this courtyard when they have been wiped out by severe winters elsewhere. Rich blue hydrangeas cope with the shade along the sides and lemon trees sit in the glass planters to be replaced by bay obelisks in the winter. The planting has to be strong to hold its own against the architecture, but the palette is rich and enjoyable.

This is a place where the design has deliberately acted as a foil for the people, the activity and the Grade I architecture. The layout quietly complies with the strong symmetry of the building. The dark red sandstone and creamy York stone echo the colours of the Victorian brick and pale terracotta. The trees frame rather than mask the façade. The southern terrace works with the sculpture gallery and the grass and water follow the sunlight and give space to the old entrance. But at the same time as being courteous to its setting and uses, I hope that the space feels like a strong statement of its own time. The form of the ellipse of steps and ramps is sculptural and far from Victorian. The glass planters and lighting are unexpected and dramatic. The water is functional and playful. Design based on use and context can be understated and respectful while still retaining strength and identity.

In summer the glass cubes are planted with lemon trees and *Iris pallida* var. *dalmatica* under the liquidambar trees provides fresh colour and sculptural leaves.

HYDE PARK CORNER
LONDON

Just up the road at Hyde Park Corner, I tried the same approach – gently but stubbornly working at the need for contemporary movement across London while respecting the historic context. The challenge was to turn a nightmare of a traffic roundabout into a space that could connect the Royal Parks and be enjoyed by people on foot, horseback and bicycle.

Hyde Park Corner is the major vehicle junction in the weaving chaos of London streets. It has always been a fulcrum of movement – albeit rather idiosyncratic and eccentric. London is different in form, politics and character from its Continental counterparts. It is not a city of baroque, axial boulevards and does not have the rectilinear, military organization of the Champs Elysées or Unter den Linden. London actually feels rather anarchic. It has evolved more around the natural features of parks and the river and the oddities of private landownership than from the disciplines of defence and political ideology.

A Saxon trackway from Charing Cross used to run through Piccadilly along the dry ground above the level that the river had cut in times of high flood. The track gradually evolved into the main London road to the west. Perched on the crest of this first Thames flood terrace, Hyde Park Corner is right on this western route in and out of the city. It was the toll gate for the road out of London at the crossing between the Westbourne and Tyburn tributaries to the Thames and became the pivot of the wonderfully crooked processional route linking the Royal Palaces through the Royal Parks. In character with

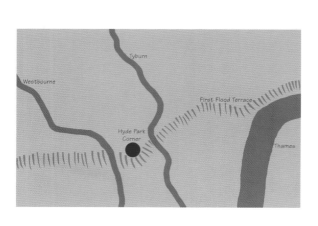

Hyde Park Corner sits at a critical nexus of routes into London from the west. It has become a symbolic space celebrating the transition from war to peace, from Empire to Commonwealth and from royal enclosure to popular landscape. The New Zealand War Memorial, opened in 2006, completes the north-eastern side of the space.

the capital, this fulcrum is in essence a green space rather than an urban plaza. The arch at the centre looks more like an ornament in a landscape park than the Arc de Triomphe or the Brandenburger Tor, and the symbolism is more to do with peace than war. The very nature of the ceremonial dog-leg at Hyde Park Corner is symbolic. It is not just a physical change of direction. It represents a change of attitude from war to peace; from Empire to Commonwealth; and from royal enclosure to popular landscape.

Although Hyde Park Corner is the crucial link in the sequence of public open spaces right across London, 1960s road engineering and a maze of intimidating subways did not encourage people through the area. The crude curve of asphalt around the Wellington Arch and the confusion of underground passages were hostile to anyone not in a vehicle. Everything had been designed for the car.

Landownership in London is complicated. Over the centuries, responsibility for the administration and maintenance of royal lands has been gradually transferred to various government bodies through a series of intricate acts. Hyde Park Corner falls between the tectonic plates of the Crown Estate, the Department for Culture, Media and Sport, Westminster City Council, Transport for London, the Royal Parks, the Greater London Authority, English Heritage and London Underground, among others. In 2000 English Heritage, who had taken over responsibility for the Wellington Arch, rather bravely set up a steering committee to do something about Hyde Park Corner and put the project out to competition.

The Hyde Park Corner Royal Artillery Memorial by Charles Sargeant Jagger is deeply moving, capturing the human devastation of the First World War.

There have probably been as many *grands projets* suggested for Hyde Park Corner as Trafalgar Square. Robert Adam made designs for the area in 1778, Aston Webb proposed a new processional route in 1901 and Edwin Lutyens came up with a plan for a vast formal plaza at the intersection in 1937. But there seems to be a national allergy to monumental urban statements. Although the Mall and Constitution Hill have been formalized, the general incremental and haphazard way that the city has evolved is part of its charm and its success. English Heritage recognized three very important things: that there was no money; that the grander the *projet*, the less likely the support; and that a coordinated sequence of short- and long-term projects would be more practical and achievable than a single assault.

The Royal Parks Review, chaired by Dame Jennifer Jenkins with Sir Terry Farrell, had already achieved a major breakthrough by allowing pedestrians to cross over to the space on the surface, rather than in underground subways. My proposal was to extend this principle, making the place welcoming to pedestrians and horses, while still allowing cars and buses to flow around the perimeter. The first step was to remove the 1960s road layout, open the gates through the Arch on the ceremonial route and fill in the subway to Green Park. The second step was to make a space where people would like to linger – a peaceful eddy off a strong flow. Although besieged by traffic, Hyde Park Corner actually has a surprising number of intrinsic advantages. It is a nexus between open spaces with its own tube station very close to the surface. It lies on a pronounced south-west-facing slope,

Hyde Park Corner remains one of the great junctions of London, but now pedestrians and horses are able to cross and enjoy the space protected from vehicles.

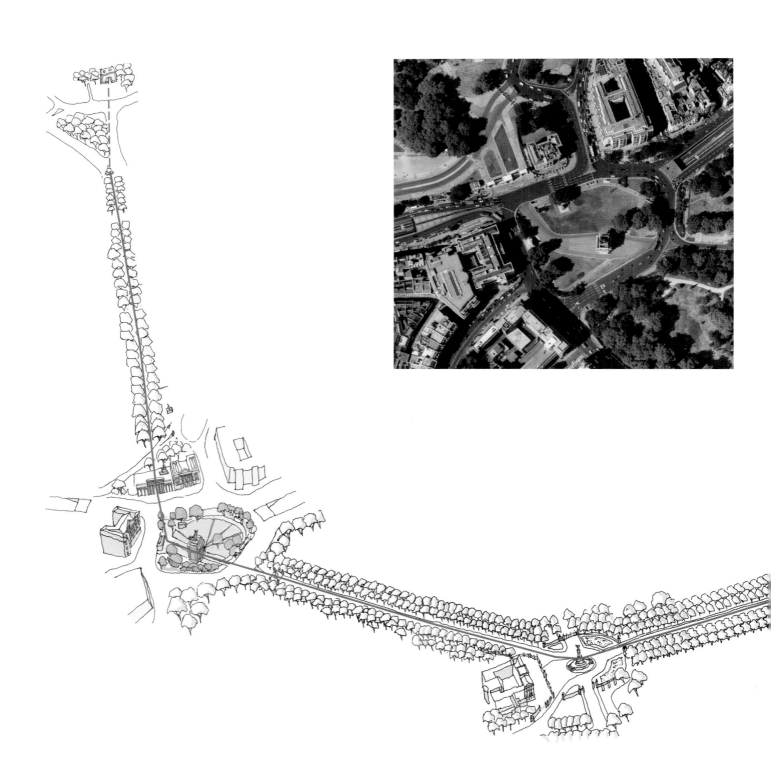

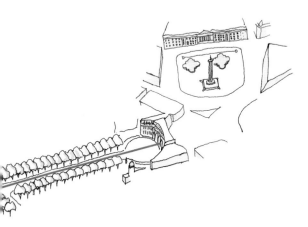

Hyde Park Corner is a fulcrum in the typically eccentric ceremonial dog-leg of London. The space, which used to be dominated by vehicles and traffic layouts, has now been softened to create a green, pedestrian place linking the Royal Parks and memorializing peace.

with excellent afternoon and evening sun. And it has the most moving war memorials in London.

Apart from inaccessibility, the problem has always been noise, pollution and the dominance of traffic. The space is surprisingly generous – over 1.5 hectares (3.7 acres) – and the proposal was to screen out the vehicles and modify the landform to help create a comfortable place to meet and linger. To the south-west I proposed building a curving wall to hold the space and block out the traffic from Victoria. To the north-east, I suggested raising the land in a gentle grass bank. These have now been achieved. The last main elements to complete are the sculpting of the central space to create a more receptive concave landform; the creation of a new parade ground south of Apsley House, relocating the mounted statue of Wellington to its centre; and the opening of the tube station out into a café restaurant to encourage people to eat and relax in the space.

Negotiation and consultation with the authorities and local groups are an essential part of a project of this complexity that continue over decades. Equally where there is no money, as is often the case with public projects, you have to be imaginative with thoughts on funding. This is not always acknowledged as the responsibility of the designer, but I have found that where you want to make major changes in the public realm you have to become involved in politics, finance and inventive lobbying. This was certainly the case with the Thames Landscape Strategy. At Hyde Park Corner, Philip Davies of English Heritage and I approached the Australian and New Zealand High Commissions, who were looking for sites for war memorials, and proposed that Hyde Park Corner might be an appropriate location. The coincidence of ambitions for the space made the projects possible.

Hyde Park Corner still has a way to go, but it is already a more comfortable and popular place than it was in 2000. The project really brought home to me how relatively small incremental changes within the flow of the possible can make real differences to urban life. The big gesture is not always necessary, possible or even desirable.

HYDE ABBEY GARDEN
WINCHESTER

At a much smaller scale, a new park in Winchester has managed a similar reconciliation between history, movement and gathering. The park was made on the site of a twelfth-century Benedictine monastery at Hyde. The abbey was built just outside the city walls and almost rivalled the cathedral in scale and wealth.

Winchester was the royal city of Alfred the Great but the bones of the king, who founded the city in AD 880, were peripatetic. Alfred was buried in the Old Minster of Winchester in 889, was moved to the New Minster in 903, then moved again in 1110 with his wife Ealhswith and his son Edward the Elder to Hyde Abbey, and then rudely disinterred after the cultural revolution of Henry VIII levelled Hyde Abbey church to the ground. The site disappeared under prison grounds and was later converted to a municipal car park.

The ruins of one of the great sacred sites in England had been all but forgotten under the cars, until excavations in 1999 revealed the foundations of the church and the empty graves of Alfred and his family. The local residents took a keen interest in the excavations and then lobbied Winchester Museum Service to keep the site open, rather than return the area to car parking. An extraordinary collaboration between the local residents and Winchester City Council then ensued. They came together to agree on a competition for a plan to remove the cars and create a new park that would link Hyde back to the cathedral. I won the competition with a simple plan that remembered the church beneath the ground and opened the space for people to use.

The whole project was made possible by the relentless energy of a remarkable local resident. Barbara Hall set up the Friends of Hyde Abbey Gardens and devoted more than five years of her life to getting the project approved, funded and built. Local authority car parks are gold dust. They bring in good revenue and demand for parking in city centres

The glass panel of Hyde Abbey church by Tracey Sheppard shows the final resting place of Alfred the Great. A garden has been carved out of a municipal car park and created over the ruins of the church. The columns and ledger stones in the glass panel line up with the features in the garden to help people imagine the lost building that the space commemorates.

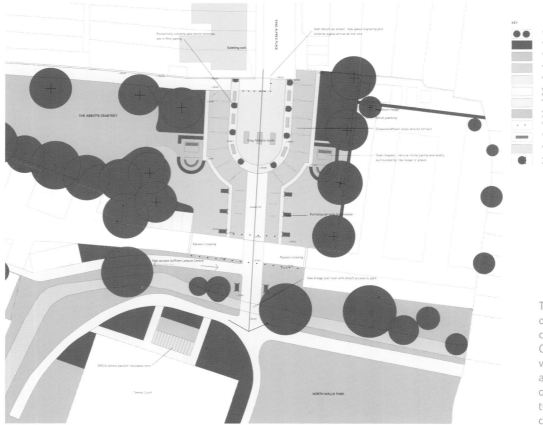

The former car park hid the remains of the sacred site and local residents combined with Winchester City Council to create a small garden where residents can pause and sit on a new link across the city. Cylinders of holly, girded with steel, mark the positions of the Saxon church columns (RIGHT).

is insatiable. So to give up car space to help fund a local park, and to allow local residents to take over an area of public land, is a brave departure for a local authority. Hyde Abbey Garden is testimony to how collaboration between a local community and its government can work.

The design for the park is deliberately uncomplicated and easy to maintain. The ruins of the abbey church are picked out as a modern garden of flint, gravel and stone above the foundations. Native plantings of oak, hazel and yew frame the space and great cylinders of holly girded with stainless steel repeat the positions of the church columns. The memory of the church can be glimpsed through a glass panel created by Tracey Sheppard, a glass engraver and local resident. The glass panel superimposes an impression of the twelfth-century church on the holly columns and layout of the foundations. Oak benches are inspired by seats in the cathedral and extend to create an axial bridge over the river. Huge ledger stones mark the graves of Alfred and his family.

The little park has become a focus for the neighbourhood and a popular gathering place on the path to the centre of the city. Because the funding, construction, planting and now the ongoing maintenance have in large part been undertaken by local residents, there is a strong sense of ownership and pride in the place. When vandals smashed the glass panel in 2010, local donations were raised in record time to make and engrave a replacement.

CITY OF LONDON CEMETERY

LONDON

Although we tend to think of social spaces in terms of urban squares or public parks, cemeteries are another kind of very important community landscape. Not only are they places where strangers are brought together in a common mood of grieving and remembering. They are also the places for a continuing relationship with the dead, or at least our vibrant memories of them – another kind of community that we have become clumsy at dealing with.

One of my more unusual commissions was for the City of London Cemetery. By 1856 the City had run out of burial space in central London and there were concerns for hygiene and sanitation within the confines of its crowded 106 parishes. It was decided to make a new cemetery on 81 hectares (200 acres) of land at Manor Park in the East End of London. One hundred and fifty years later this cemetery is once again running out of space and my brief was wonderfully brief: 'Design a way to bury the dead in the coming century that is sustainable in terms of space, energy, dignity and financial viability.'

The City of London Cemetery now covers 81 hectares (200 acres) of trees, lawns and shrubberies, but there is a hidden corner that has been used as a rubbish tip for nearly a hundred years, gradually growing higher and spreading wider. The tip is concealed behind high trees and banks and has served a useful function, but with advances in recycling, and pressure on burial space, it is something of a wasted asset.

The City of London Cemetery at Manor Park.

The green waste site for the new burial ground.

The Corporation of the City of London has been very advanced in its attitude to death, welcoming all denominations and burial choices, including catacombs, where coffins are placed on shelves above one another, and columbaria, where cremation urns are secreted. The Corporation provided the first crematorium in Greater London in 1902. As space becomes more limited and populations increase, the Corporation is open to new ideas for dealing with our dead. One of the problems is that cemeteries are very expensive to maintain and by their nature, the people who funded their graves are no longer around when the stones begin to collapse in a rather mobile soil a few decades later.

The unusual character of this site called for an unorthodox solution. A century of green waste piled 5 metres (16 feet) high in a long narrow strip needed sorting out. Traditional graves or tombstones would not work in such an unstable, inappropriate soil, but the raised ground surrounded by tall trees suggested that a landform solution might work. At the same time, I was taken by the dual nature of a cemetery. On the one hand it is a place for solitary contemplation of eternity. On the other it is an area where the dead are laid out together in space-efficient patterns not dissimilar from town plans. We take our urban layouts with us to the grave to create strikingly similar neighbourhoods in death – and probably complain just as much about the designs and ornamentations of our neighbours. Medieval churchyards have a dense and organic pattern that resembles their villages. The Cemetery of Père-Lachaise in Paris was deliberately laid out like elegant Parisian streets. Lawn and woodland cemeteries mirror our desire for garden and sylvan suburbs. How should we think about our cities for the dead and the living in the coming century?

Carbon and recycling are pressing issues. Cremation solves the problem of space but requires intense energy and for some religions has uncomfortable associations with hellfire. The Romans understood how quickly and cleanly a dead body decomposes if it is not sealed away. Catacombs and ossuaries (where the bones from the catacombs were later assembled together) were highly effective ways of dealing with lack of space and low energy requirements. They also form stable structures that do not require intense maintenance to cope with subsidence. The problem was how to create a burial ground that worked in such an efficient, simple and sustainable way that also spoke to the English love of space, greenery and contemplation of nature.

After a great deal of research and advice from the excellent engineers Integral, I proposed reforming the long, curving space into a landscape of rolling grass mounds which ripple down across the site, surrounded by an elevated terrace walk. The dip faces of the rolling mounds are continuously grassy while the scarps are vertical faces of slate and stone, giving access to the burial chambers. Looking out eastwards from the high point of the cemetery, all you will see is undulating grass stretching down to the Wanstead flats. Approaching from

The nineteenth-century catacombs immediately to the north of the site.

the east a series of curving stone faces will lead you to each tomb. Catacombs, columbaria and crypts will be built into the mounds. The boundary will be defined by ramparts that also rise and fall. The top will be broad enough to accommodate a path and standing memorials.

The idea draws on the Orkney long barrows and the sacred landscape of Salisbury Plain with its distant perspectives over simple grass and sky, punctuated by burial mounds and standing stones.

The Director of the City of London Cemetery, Ian Hussein, was amazingly receptive to the rather unorthodox ideas for the new burial ground. With all the earth moving and structural work needed for the mounds and tombs, the capital investment is nevertheless daunting and the project has not yet started.

The proposed new burial mounds inspired by the Orkney long barrows that will house catacombs, columbaria and crypts.

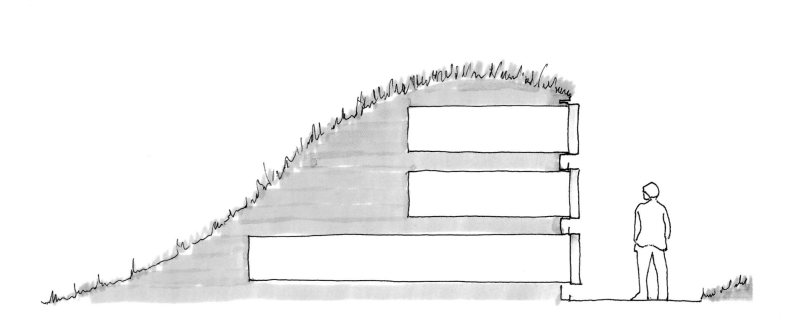

The burial mounds wind down through the site, flanked by descending ramparts. From the south visitors will look out over a field of rippling wildflowers with the curving stone faces of the mounds approached from the north east.

Franklin Farm, Hampshire.

SPIRIT

The spirit of the land carries many names and beliefs – from a biosphere of related habitats to ley lines to Mother Earth, we attribute a connected living wholeness to the planet. At some level landscape architecture has to address this and reach beyond the responsibilities and practicalities summed up by Alexander Pope as 'use' to try to grasp the 'genius of the place'. This 'genius' is only partly based in physical characteristics – topography, aspect, climate and vegetation – it also covers the memories and associations that have accumulated in that spot. In other words it is the personality, identity or spirit of the place.

Design needs to respond to local identity and draw inspiration from the memories of the place in order to voice its spirit. To some extent the process is intuitive. You need to listen and absorb.

At its best, design understands the idea of a place, giving it a physical form that can make past, present and future simultaneous. The JFK Memorial at Runnymede is a good example. It captures spirit in the most subtle but effective way.

THIS ACRE OF ENGLISH GROUND WAS GIVEN
TO THE UNITED STATES OF AMERICA BY
THE PEOPLE OF BRITAIN IN MEMORY OF
JOHN F. KENNEDY
PRESIDENT OF THE UNITED STATES 1961-63
DIED BY AN ASSASSINS HAND 22 NOVEMBER 1963

The John F. Kennedy Memorial at Runneymede was designed by the English landscape architect Sir Geoffrey Jellicoe. The place is an east-facing hillside on the Thames river terrace west of London. It is a charming but unremarkable spot and typical of much of the Thames Valley. A busy road runs through the water meadow down beside the river. The memorial itself is simple: a sequence of fifty meandering, rough-cut steps leading up through woodland to a small glade overlooking the river. On the platform a stone memorial tablet to President Kennedy is inscribed with a quote from his inaugural address: 'Let every Nation know, whether it wishes us well or ill, that we shall pay any price, bear any burden, meet any hardship, support any friend or oppose any foe, in order to assure the survival and success of liberty.'

Despite the modest normalness of the setting and the simplicity of the stone tablet, this is a place of power and beauty. It is charged with deep beliefs of our culture in democracy, equality and freedom under law. The JFK Memorial was inaugurated by Queen Elizabeth and Jacqueline Kennedy in May 1965, just eighteen months after his assassination, and the land that it stands on was given by the British people to the United States of America. This whole valley has significance. Down below, on an island in the Thames, the open-air council of the Anglo-Saxon kings, the Witangemot, used to be held and 500 years later, in 1215, Magna Carta was sealed on the same island by King John. The place symbolizes liberty. But there is more going on here than a history lesson. I believe that you could walk those steps without knowing all the stories and still be profoundly moved. The number of feet that have trodden the path and the intensity of the emotions they have felt are somehow tangible. The spirit of a place shrinks time and resonates with everything ever felt there.

Jellicoe designed steps to follow the slope of the land, avoid tree roots and use 60,000 hand-cut granite setts, laid straight into the soil. The design is such a light touch that you hardly notice that a designer has been involved, and the effect is at once gentle and subtly strong. It is a comfortable climb that encourages you to concentrate on the trees, the light and the rhythm of walking. You reach the glade unexpectedly and the power of the words is undiluted. The complete simplicity and unpretentiousness of the sequence is in harmony with everything it represents.

INSPIRATION

The magical forms of tumuli rising through autumn mist have stirred English imaginations from Spenser to Hardy to Ravilious. Viking barrows, sacred circles and earth mazes form a deep sediment of landscape memory in the national mind. Early earthworks were carefully placed on ridges or knolls to take full advantage of the strategic view and make maximum impact from a distance. Their presences still dominate the landscape millennia later. Even when the earthworks were defensive rather than sacred, such as Maiden Castle, Offa's Dyke or even Palmerston's anti-Napoleonic redoubts, they were brilliant land sculptures.

Ironically earth forms tend to survive even longer than buildings and are repeatedly reappropriated. Burial mounds, such as the one in Richmond Park, have been reused as hunting high points and communication lookouts. The Richmond Park mound aligns with St Paul's Cathedral and is now named King Henry's Mount. Henry VIII supposedly waited there for the signal from the Tower that Anne Boleyn had been beheaded and he could ride off to marry number three. The Thames landscape was dotted with similar viewing mounds. Francis Bacon created mounts at Twickenham Park in the seventeenth century and during the eighteenth century, a whole series of mounds were raised along the river, notably for Princess Caroline at Richmond Lodge and Alexander Pope in Twickenham.

Sculpting the earth is one of the most dramatic ways of designing in the landscape and it is fun. The subtlety of the form, often hidden in flat light, can become powerful at dawn or dusk or in frost and low mist. With the possibility of different patterns of grasses, grazing or mowing, the scope it offers for imaginative design seems infinite. A few of these historic landforms have been particular inspiration for me.

AVEBURY RING

Avebury Ring is a Neolithic henge monument of three concentric stone circles in Wiltshire constructed around 2600 BC. Although Stonehenge receives all the Oscars, there is something just as powerful about Avebury Ring, the more so for being quietly unexpected. The village has encroached into the centre of the ring and roads run through the middle. The stones are humbler and more quizzical and sheep munch away over the whole site. Somehow the integration of subsequent life into the rings of stones makes them feel less set apart – more connected to our relationship with the land. Wandering up and down the banks and ditches, without fully understanding the 5,000 years of significance, and looking across to the huge Silbury Hill you feel part of a very long story. There is connection without full comprehension and enormous pleasure in the lumpy geometry of a place that still somehow feels sacred.

RIDGE AND FURROW

There is nothing sacred about ridge and furrow. It is the result of centuries of practical ploughing through the Middle Ages in Britain. From the post-Roman period through to the seventeenth century, regular ploughs turned the soil over to the right and tilled the land clockwise in rectangular strips. Over time this heaped the soil up into parallel ridges separated by troughs or furrows. Modern mechanical ploughing can till in both directions simultaneously and removes these patterns, but where medieval arable land was turned to pasture, the underlying shapes survive, especially in the English Midlands. The forms are extremely subtle, usually no more than 60 centimetres (2 feet) in height between the ridge and the furrow. In most lights the fields just look flat, but then suddenly evening shadows or ground frost will pick out a comfortable corduroy stretched over the surface of the land. The beauty of the pattern comes partly from parallel light and shadow over an irregular plane; partly from the surprise being revealed by a transient moment of weather; and partly from knowing that this subtle form represented centuries of patient management of the land and fed generation after generation of settlers. There is a further aspect that especially appeals to me. When I look at land I shrink the scale and imagine running my fingers over the surface, feeling and stroking the shapes. Ridge and furrow feels great to the touch.

LYVEDEN NEW BIELD

There is a strange difference between a ruin and an unfinished building. After a few years they look much the same, but the incomplete building is still full of the optimism of construction as opposed to the melancholy of destruction in a ruin. Lyveden New Bield is a half-completed stone house in Northamptonshire that was abandoned in 1605 when Sir Thomas Tresham died and his son became embroiled in the Gunpowder Plot to blow up Parliament. To the side of the house is the garden Sir Thomas was also planning. On an intimate domestic scale moats, ramparts, mounds and orchards wait half-completed along with the stone building. There is none of the clutter of furnishings, plants or statues — just the purity of grass, stone and water. In the flat Northamptonshire countryside the empty windows and reflecting canals capture light in a magical way. It is a place of expectation and imagination, full of hope rather than memory.

ROUSHAM

I keep returning to three particular gardens from the first half of the eighteenth century: Rousham in Oxfordshire, Claremont in Surrey and Studley Royal in Yorkshire. These places seem to distil landform and water to pure spirit. Rousham manages to be wonderfully domestic. The parkland is grazed by Longhorn cattle and chickens scatter in the stableyard as you search for the honesty box to pay to enter the garden of what is still the Cottrell-Dormer family home. I first visited Rousham very early on a perfect summer morning. There was no one else around and we were able to amble along the narrow serpentine paths and discover one hidden surprise after another. Rousham was designed by Charles Bridgeman and then overlaid by William Kent. The strength of Bridgeman's design, suspending the gardens above the River Cherwell, gives a clarity that enabled Kent to create a series of delightful eddies in the flow. Kent was evoking the themes of Augustan poetry and classical Arcadia, but you don't need to know any of this to enjoy his temples, pools and grottos. The best of all is a narrow stone rill that meanders gracefully through woodland before flowing into an octagonal reflecting pool in a glade above the river. The subtlety of the light on the slightly turbulent rill turning into a mirror plane of reflecting water in the octagon is mesmerizing. The rill and pool are set in bare, swept earth under trees.

CLAREMONT

Kent also followed Bridgeman at Claremont, though the scale is much grander. When I first saw an illustration of Bridgeman's grass amphitheatre for Claremont, I thought the painter had had problems with the perspective, but it really is like that. Grass terraces fan and curve over 1.2 hectares (3 acres) in the most extraordinarily bold shapes and planes. Bridgeman carved in earth and turf the way that a sculptor chisels wood or stone. To the east of the amphitheatre, Kent made a beautiful serpentine ha-ha but unfortunately he naturalized the octagonal pool that Bridgeman designed at the base of the amphitheatre. The concentric rings of the grass terraces descending to an octagonal reflecting lake must have been very powerful when they were first made.

The moon ponds at Studley Royal are serene distillations of geometry and reflection. The simple shapes are cut cleanly out of turf, deep in the valley of the River Skell, and reflect the trees, temple and sky in fractured patterns. The best way to approach Studley Royal is from the cascade to the south. The perfect proportions of the framing lodges and cascade lead you on to the moon ponds and it is only having glimpsed the ruined Fountains Abbey to the north that you should progress from the sculptural balance of the eighteenth century to the rugged destruction of the sixteenth. The whole sequence shows the relationship between water, landform and philosophy in a beautiful and calm way. Studley Royal was created by John Aislabie after his disgrace in the South Sea Bubble financial scandal. Aislabie's expulsion from Parliament and disqualification from public life released him to create one of the finest gardens in England.

The Temple of Piety seen across the moon and half-crescent ponds at Studley Royal.

ANDY GOLDSWORTHY

These historic examples of inspiration are mostly to show the depth and variety of the earthwork tradition in the British Isles. But earthworking is still very much alive. Some of the most imaginative new directions have been led by environmental artists such as Andy Goldsworthy and Richard Long. Andy Goldsworthy's *Taking a Wall for a Walk* in the Grizedale Sculpture Park, for example, humorously combines memory of the old field patterns with a sensuous form that weaves between the trees and land. Over centuries, the open Cumbrian hillsides had been painstakingly groomed of stones that were collected into walls to contain sheep. As the fields at Grizedale fell into neglect, the walls began to collapse and larch forests were planted. The forest was then turned into a sculpture park. Andy Goldsworthy wove all three histories together in the most simple and imaginative way.

I first saw Andy Goldworthy's work in the Serpentine Gallery in the 1980s. Although I have spent my life looking at nature, Andy Goldsworthy always makes me see things completely afresh. From understanding the ephemeral delicacy of leaves and twigs to the rough beauty of ice and rock, he has managed to keep the open eyes of childhood that you usually lose with age. And he carries on exploring, imagining and helping us to see. *Taking a Wall for a Walk* is a most eloquent expression of how to absorb history, use and spirit — and create beautiful wit. This is poetry and landscape and observation at their most direct and unselfconscious.

I have given a very personal reaction to these inspiring places, but Bridgeman's landforms at Claremont, set beside Aislabie's moon ponds at Studley Royal, reveal a tradition which has re-emerged more generally in contemporary landscape design, such as Charles Jencks's and Maggie Keswick's work at Portrack, and is now inspiring mounds and earthworks throughout Europe. Across the Atlantic in the United States, earthworks have also drawn on a separate tradition of native American design. The materials, scale and light are often different, tending to work with massive rock projects in desert areas. Smithson's spiral jetty and the work of James Turrell continue to inspire. Some earthworks in the United States are also clothed with grass, very much in the English tradition. At his farm in Maine, James Pierce has consciously drawn on burial mounds, military redoubts and turf mazes to create a series of sculptural earthworks. And Maya Lin's work from the Vietnam Veterans' Memorial to the Storm King Wavefield is breathtakingly beautiful.

In addition to earthworks, the United States has been a major source of inspiration. I was very fortunate to study under Michael Laurie at the University of California in Berkeley and the work of Thomas Church and Dan Kiley still leave me in awe. But one particular place stands out above all the rest. When I was eighteen I visited New York. I had travelled to London on a few occasions, but this was the first time I had really been in a full-on city. By the third day my head was exploding and a friend took me down East 53rd Street and then suddenly off the street into Paley Park. I felt rescued. That was probably the moment I decided to become a landscape architect – although I had no notion that the profession existed and didn't realize what had happened until nearly five years later. The space is only 390 square metres (4,200 square feet), the footprint of one of the buildings that William Paley replaced with a private park, open to the people. The design is incredibly simple – granite setts on the ground, walls of ivy and falling water, a ceiling of honey locusts, wire mesh chairs and a few brightly planted concrete pots – yet the place is tranquil, alive and an amazing refuge in a super-charged city. Designed by Zion & Breen in 1967, this is probably still one of the most innovative urban spaces in the world.

LANDFORM

From an early age I have been obsessed with landforms and I seem to have ended up in the right place for the obsession. As the previous examples show, Britain is a fine country for earthworks. The climate, the geology and the topography make soil and grass remarkably durable and expressive materials. Rain helps abundant grass to grow; sheep and rabbits can keep the surface short and smooth; and the low northern light shows off the subtle shapes at dawn and dusk.

The fan of grass terraces behind Heveningham Hall responds to the flow of the land, retains the old trees and gives the house room to breathe.

One of my first projects at Heveningham Hall in Suffolk involved massive movements of soil. Behind the hall the land rises sharply to the south and the garden front has always posed a problem. Even the brothers La Rochefoucauld, visiting shortly after construction at the end of the eighteenth century, complained that it was an unsuccessful space. A typical Victorian parterre had been built on the site in 1877, but the scale and ornamentation jarred beside the 80 metre (87 yard) long Georgian façade and retaining walls blocked the views from the main reception rooms. The registered garden beside the Grade I listed house was clumsy for its setting, shaky in its foundations and, to be honest, not a very good design. In a groundbreaking decision, English Heritage consented to demolition of the parterre and replacement with a completely new garden of sweeping grass terraces.

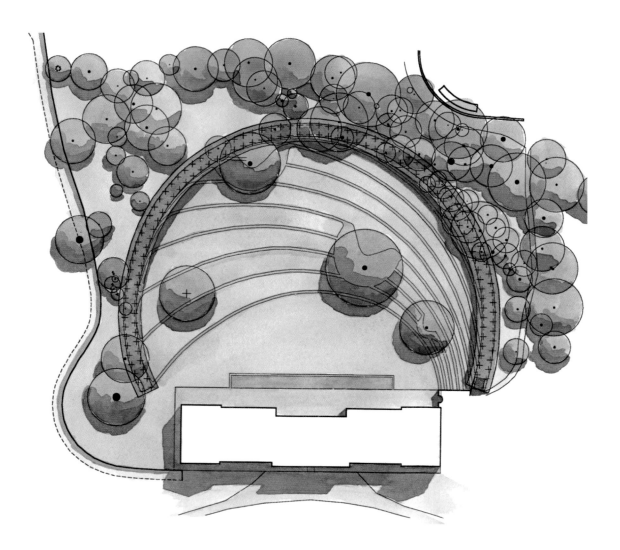

Sketching away on the draughting table, I designed a symmetrical pattern of grass steps, responding to the purity of the house. But on returning to the site, it was clear that the underlying slopes were doing something quite different. The ground rises at an angle off to the south-west and cuts back to the service yard beside the house. After a lot of puzzling, I let the land lead the design. The terraces flow with the rising ground, fanning out in a Golden Section spiral curves (see page 155). The geometry is broken by grassy domes over the root plates of the veteran oaks and cedars that predated the parterre. A symmetrical arc of holm oaks shade the walk that contains the terraces and retains a balance with the house, rising gently with the natural slope and descending down steps into the service yard to the west. A 5 x 50 metre (16 x 165 foot) reflecting canal links the house terrace to the lawns and makes a great lap pool. The design was inspired by the landform, the setting of the hall and the scale of the landscape. It has tried to shed the mistakes of the past and yet respond to the needs and memories of the place.

The design is based on the flow of the Golden Section spiral, rising 9 metres (30 feet) to the south-west, enclosed by an arc of holm oaks and connected to the house terrace by a 50 metre (165 foot) reflecting pool.

GREAT FOSTERS
SURREY

At Great Fosters in Surrey the problems were different. Great Fosters has had many lives: from a moated, seventeenth-century Windsor Great Park hunting lodge; to one of the houses that belonged to the family that adopted Jane Austen's brother; to an aristocratic lunatic asylum; to the first country house hotel on the Ascot and debutante circuit, celebrated by Noël Coward in *Relative Values*. The elaborate Arts and Crafts gardens have been restored by the owners, but in 1972 the M25 amputated the last third of the axial avenue and exposed the Grade I building to the noise and fumes of the congested motorway. The whole garden focuses on this axial vista and the place felt ripped apart.

After years of discussions with the Highways Agency and acquisition of the neighbouring fields, we were able to find the funds to build 800 metres (half a mile) of protective earth bunds and a 6 metre (20 foot) high grass amphitheatre as the new terminus to the avenue. The sculptural landform reduces the noise and hides the motorway at the same time as giving a focal end to the axial vista. To celebrate the opening we held a concert with a string quartet, just 25 metres (27 yards) from the busiest motorway in the country. The acoustic was perfect.

The restored Arts and Crafts garden at Great Fosters where the axial vista had been amputated by the M25 motorway in 1972.

At the truncated end of the vista we built a grass amphitheatre flanked by an 800 metre (half a mile) long bund to conceal the motorway and protect the garden from the traffic. The acoustic is so good that string quartets can play only 25 metres (82 feet) away from the traffic.

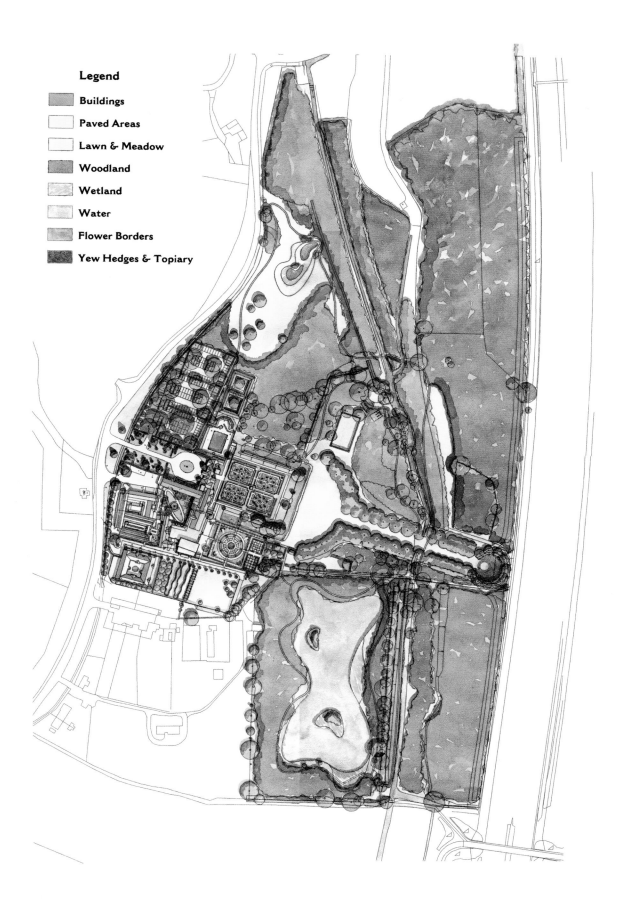

Legend

- Buildings
- Paved Areas
- Lawn & Meadow
- Woodland
- Wetland
- Water
- Flower Borders
- Yew Hedges & Topiary

The courtyard of the old County Hall has been similarly transformed. The old concrete roof grate in the centre of the court has been turned into a turf sculpture. Weight restrictions led to some unorthodox use of polystyrene as subsoil and growth mats for vertical grass faces, but the final result is a kind of ziggurat of turf in a hard and austere urban space.

We have reinstated the old 1930s system of suspending a central light off wires from the building and the turf sculpture glows green through the archway to Westminster Bridge.

The turf sculpture at the entrance to the former County Hall in London.

Holker Hall is spectacularly sited in the southern Lake District on the edge of Morecambe Bay. The house has been in the family since 1756, and is still lived in by the Cavendishes. The estate has survived as a lively modern enterprise, open to the public and working energetically with its woodland, venison, salt marsh lamb and slate quarries.

The parkland stretching down towards the bay is particularly fine and Lord and Lady Cavendish have created a famous garden around the house with rare collections of trees and shrubs. The visitor car park and shop, however, sat rather awkwardly on the slope above the house in a broad expanse of asphalt that reached almost to the front door.

In 2000 I was asked to help produce a long-term masterplan for the grounds around the hall. The first and most urgent step was to tackle the unfortunate car park. Working with the characteristic topography of the parkland, we created a kind of woodland bowl for the cars, scooping up a huge fold of land to separate the parking from the house. The drive was realigned to approach the hall more gracefully and the visitor entrance diverted to flow in a series of gently rising loops through the trees. We were able to take advantage of the Burlington slate from the estate and create sinuous parking areas of green slate mulch with riven slate details along the road edge.

The Holker Hall car park has been folded into the land to hide the cars from the wider landscape.

The car park now feels as though it sits more peacefully on the land and the sculptural curves create glades of oak trees that have become popular for picnics. Even the most utilitarian of spaces can be attractive if it flows sympathetically with the land beneath, rather than dominating the setting.

The family house has evolved through fashions, fires and family taste and its garden has changed in step. Hugh and Grania Cavendish continue to alter and refine the garden layout. The latest project has been to remove an unfortunate nineteenth-century roadway that sliced through the middle of the garden and return the land to its underlying slopes. The roadway was perplexingly incongruous. It started and finished in nothing and cut across the flow of the rest of the garden. In its place we have moulded the space into a cupped grass glade, with a glimpse out towards Morecambe Bay. The glade is surrounded by limes, eucryphias and cercidiphyllum forming a kind of pagan grove on the meandering circuit around the garden.

The new pagan grove at Holker Hall creates the imprint of an egg in the grass and is surrounded by a special collection of limes, eucryphias and bulbs.

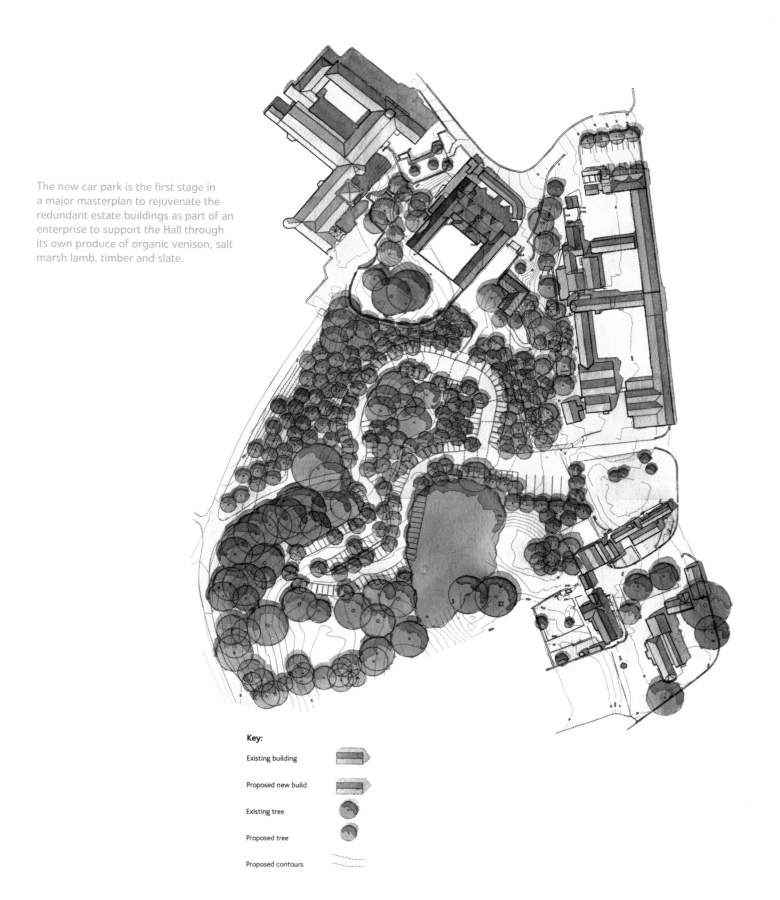

The new car park is the first stage in a major masterplan to rejuvenate the redundant estate buildings as part of an enterprise to support the Hall through its own produce of organic venison, salt marsh lamb, timber and slate.

Key:

Existing building

Proposed new build

Existing tree

Proposed tree

Proposed contours

HURSTBOURNE PARK
HAMPSHIRE

Landforms can be minimal as well as monumental. The house at Hurstbourne Park is the third on the site since the eighteenth century. It sits on the crest of a dramatic chalk valley that descends southwards through wooded parkland. The idea was to connect the house as directly as possible to the views to north and south, keeping more intimate and flower gardens off to the west.

An old ha-ha provided the perfect transition to the southern parkland but there was a desire for some relief between the house terrace and the ha-ha. It was important not to interrupt the view and so I proposed a subtle knot garden of turf cut down into the grass. It is only really in morning and evening light that the shapes of the garden emerge as a modern sculpture, but it is a good place for children to roll and play, and blends easily with the scale of the valley beyond.

A gentle turf knot garden makes the transition between the house and its parkland.

THE HOLT
HAMPSHIRE

Many houses built in the seventeenth century were careful to position themselves in the lee of the south-westerly prevailing wind, tucked under north east-facing slopes to protect them from the weather. As the houses became grander, heating easier and glass more affordable, the fashion for views and southern light changed priorities. Houses that had been sited for sound environmental reasons found that their gardens did not work for the new relationship with the outdoors. A number of places such as Claremont took the radical decision to demolish the old house and rebuild on a high sunlit ridge. For others, including Heveningham, the houses were altered and walled gardens were constructed off to the side, but the main south-facing gardens remained compromised and overshadowed by steep slopes.

The Holt is a lovely seventeenth-century six-bay house with its garden front tucked into a steep slope. Over the years attempts had been made to carve out tennis courts and random level areas in the looming ground to the south and east, but this had emphasized rather than eased the awkwardness of the setting. Extensions to the house had exacerbated the problem with ground levels over half a metre (20 inches) above the internal floors. Three hundred years after the house was built, the next generation decided to try to sort out the problem properly.

The new grass terraces carved out of the land behind the seventeenth-century house.

The south-eastern slope was drawn back to allow light and space to the garden front of the house.

The grass terraces descend to a zig-zag
path that links the library door with the
gate to the viewing mound.

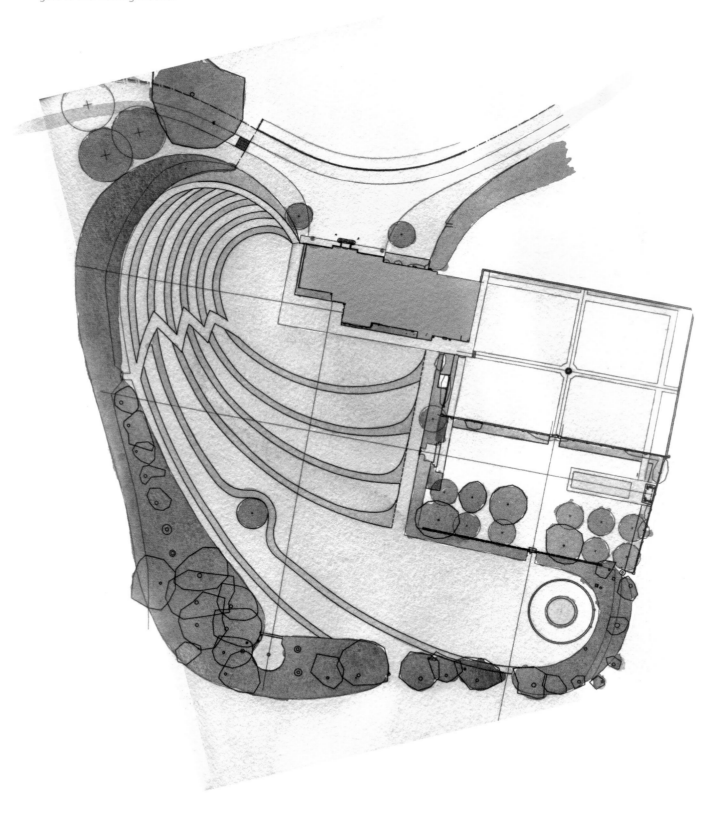

The pattern rotates around the house.

In order to give the house space to breathe and make room for generous stone terraces, we had to move huge amounts of chalk. The design creates two descending wings of fanned grass terraces, intersecting in a zig-zag that leads up to an old wrought-iron gate through perimeter yews. The wings mimic a bird in turning flight, with the zig-zag as a spine.

Just beyond the grass terraces, the owners' grandmother had laid out a series of avenues radiating from a circular space. We used the chalk spoil to make a 5 metre (16 foot) high spiral grass mound at the centre of the avenue glade. As you walk up the mound, you look along each avenue in turn and then survey the whole scene from the top, emerging into the setting sun. When you approach the house from the north drive, the bright green of the mound shines at the terminus of each avenue as you pass.

A final project will be to use the remaining spoil to make a raised circular dew pond in a clearing deeper into the woods, at the end of one of the radiating avenues.

ROTHERFIELD PARK
HAMPSHIRE

Rotherfield is one of the most perfect English parklands. The great stone house looks east over rolling chalk downland, accentuated by clumps of trees and an arched stone bridge that connects two grassy knolls and makes the entrance to the house. Across the valley the church is subtly raised on a mound so that the tower rises above the surrounding trees and village. The house itself is the closest thing to a gothick, Scottish castle in southern England and has been used as the location for a number of films.

Although the site is much older, the Grade I house was extensively remodelled in the nineteenth century. Elaborate walled gardens to the north-west are immaculately maintained and the house and parkland have been carefully tended for generations. Nevertheless, immediately to the south of the house, a lumpy area of grass sloping up to a southern ridge looked as though the builders moved out in the 1870s and left the grass to grow over their heaps of rubble. Indeed this is more or less what had happened. Ambitious schemes for an Edwardian terrace and then a dainty flower garden by Russell Page had never quite caught the imagination or the budgets of the family.

The recontoured lawn to the south of Rotherfield Park.

The house and stable block now relate
more comfortably to one another
and the view opens eastwards to the
parkland and church.

The problem remained that the best garden aspect of the house had never been resolved. The house entrance and approach are on the north front; service yards span the north-west; a dramatic ha-ha revealing views drops away to the east; yet the main lawn to the south remained lumpy and unconvincing.

The solution was to create a generous flat lawn that gave the stables and tower a level bank and base, allowing the architecture on the northern and western sides of the space to be properly grounded and relate formally to the garden. On the southern ridge things could be freer. In the carving back of the land to create the flat lawn, the slope became steeper and more dramatic. The idea was to curve the grass slope in an arc and to create a rising pleat or grass terrace, a little like a gusset in a sleeve. The transition between the end of the space and the view was more difficult. It needed a form that was strong enough to balance the towers of the castellated house and the stables as well as linking to the bold downland beyond. In the local tradition of earth fortifications and tumuli, we made a great hemispherical mound that acts as a fulcrum between the ridge and the carved slope. The views from the top are spectacular and the turf architecture is bold enough to balance the stone and brick edifices on the other two sides of the enclosed lawn.

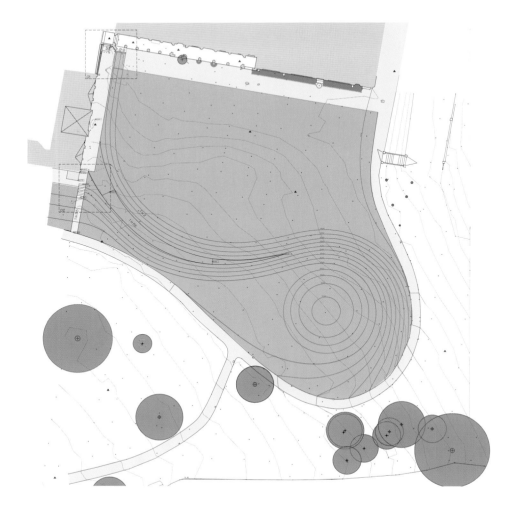

A single grass terrace rises to a
hemispherical mound in the local
tradition of earth fortifications
and tumuli.

Back in Richmond, the Thames Landscape Study threw up some particularly interesting local projects. The King's Observatory in the Old Deer Park was one of the most intriguing. The Old Deer Park has been a significant royal site since Edward III first converted the Shene manor house into a palace in the fourteenth century and created an open warren for the chase right from Shene (the original name for Richmond) to Kew. The royal presence continued through the reigns of the Tudors and the Stuarts to the Hanoverians.

In 1414 Henry V built a pair of religious foundations across the river from one another at Syon and Richmond to pray for the soul of his father. As soon as the monks in the Charterhouse finished praying, the nuns across the Thames would take over and so they would alternate for all eternity, or at least until Henry VIII dissolved the monasteries and demolished both establishments.

Richmond was a favourite palace of Elizabeth I, who called it her 'warm winter box' and retreated there to die in 1603. The Hanoverians gradually began building more modern palaces, each one edging further north towards Kew. George II and Queen Caroline were particularly keen on the Old Deer Park, but it was their son George III who commissioned William Chambers to design the King's Observatory adjacent to the remains of the old Charterhouse.

The Observatory was built very specifically to observe the transit of Venus as it came close to the Earth on 3 June 1769. Chambers built a perfect little white villa with a revolving lead dome for the telescope. The villa was set like a temple on a hemispherical

The King's Observatory at Kew was built by Sir William Chambers for George III to observe the transit of Venus in 1769. The meridian was set from this building until it moved to Greenwich in the nineteenth century.

mound in the middle of Lancelot Brown's recently smoothed parkland that stretched up to Kew and across the river to Syon in a single Arcadian landscape. The King's Observatory became a scientific focus, housing George III's collection of clocks and scientific instruments and marking the meridian until it moved to Greenwich towards the end of the nineteenth century.

George IV abandoned Richmond and Kew for Brighton but Brown's parkland and the King's Observatory survived and the Old Deer Park is still owned by the Crown Estate. The King's Observatory became a central observation centre for the New Meteorological Office in 1867, sharing the building with the National Physical Laboratory from 1900 to 1910. From 1980 the Observatory was sub-let as an office headquarters to Autoglass. The site was surrounded by a rectangle of close board fencing, and a number of new office buildings, a caretaker's flat, a swimming pool and car parks for forty-eight vehicles were built in the grounds. This rather detracted from the Arcadian setting.

The head leaseholder from the Crown is now proposing to restore the Observatory as a private dwelling. The office buildings, parking and general clutter will be removed and the accommodation hidden underground. The perimeter rectangle of close board fencing will be replaced by ha-has and groups of trees to frame the views and restore the temple-like building to its parkland landscape.

The King's Observatory lies right in the London flood plain. Every centimetre of soil has to be accounted for in this critical flood storage area. The plans therefore scoop out gentle swales and a small lake to increase flood capacity and restore the grassy mound at the base of the Observatory. The underground accommodation is arranged around a central garden courtyard that brings light and air into the dwelling with terraced fans opening at either end. The underground gardens have been designed rather playfully to mark the position of the planets at the time of the 1769 transit of Venus. The fanned terraces to north and south will be planted in the bands of Saturn and Jupiter. The centre of the garden symbolizes the sun with Mars above it and Venus and the Earth beneath. A fire pit will mark Mars and a rill and pool of water, Venus and the Earth.

The Observatory was originally set on a small mound that raised the building out of the flood plain, looking like a white temple in Lancelot Brown's Arcadian Old Deer Park.

Joseph Farington showed how the
landscapes of Kew, Syon and the Old Deer
Park blended across the river to the design
of Lancelot Brown.

Modern car parks and outhouses will be
swept away and replaced under the earth
around a courtyard designed to reflect the
relative positions of the planets at the 1769
transit of Venus.

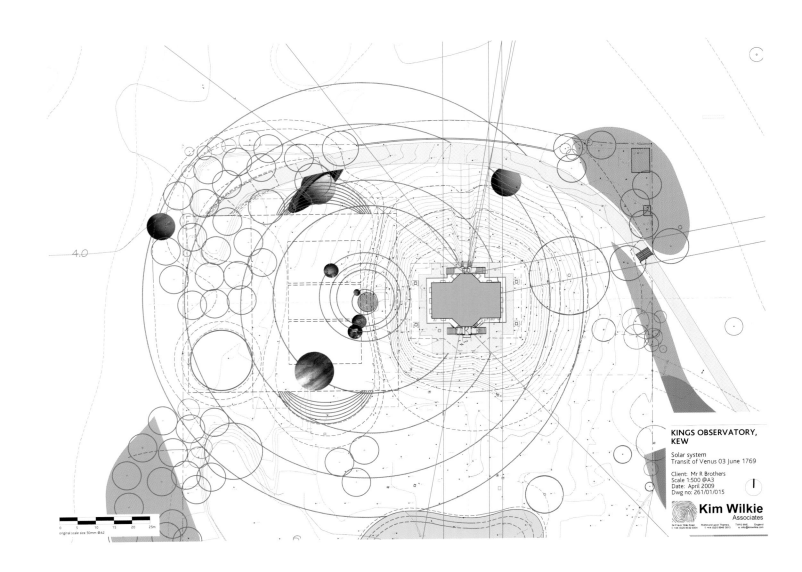

KINGS OBSERVATORY,
KEW

Solar system
Transit of Venus 03 June 1769

Client: Mr R Brothers
Scale 1:500 @A3
Date: April 2009
Dwg no: 261/01/015

Kim Wilkie
Associates

The King's Observatory is the key building in the Old Deer Park and the plans are to integrate the parkland more effectively with the river and soften the planting of the surrounding golf course, using native trees and acid grassland roughs.

BOUGHTON HOUSE
NORTHAMPTONSHIRE

I was first asked to Boughton on a morning in late spring 2004. Lord Dalkeith showed me the extent of the restoration work that he and his father were undertaking on the avenues and canals in the historic landscape and then led me up to the top of a small hill covered in sycamores and Lawson cypress. From the edge of the hill you could just see down to the crumbling banks of the River Ise and an uneven stretch of land beyond, leading up to a holly hedge and the family swimming pool 800 metres (half a mile) away. 'So what would you do with this?' he asked me.

The overgrown hill we were standing on was originally a perfect truncated grass pyramid that Bridgeman had designed in 1724 for the 2nd Duke of Montagu as a base for a mausoleum. It looked out over a 800 metre (half-mile) view, referred to on old plans as 'the hurried over' – a sequence of land that had never been fully resolved or designed, leading up to a medieval stew pond and bowling green. It was a thrilling thought: the possibility or working with one of the greatest formal landscapes in England, to design something that was inspired by both the place and its precisely calculated pattern, and also to excite the next generation.

Boughton is a sculptural landscape of avenues, canals and grass terraces created by the first two Dukes of Montagu between 1685 and 1725. The first quarter of the eighteenth century in England was one of the most stimulating stages in the history of landscape design. During the transition between the intricate formality of French baroque and the broad panoramas of English parkland, there were some bold experiments with sculptural and geometric landforms. These were quickly smoothed away by the Arcadian English Landscape Movement and very few survive. Bridgeman was the leading designer of those two remarkable decades and Boughton is one of the few of these transition landscapes to escape subsequent design fashion intact. While the family concentrated on their great Scottish estates, they left the place to fall asleep. It was not until nearly three hundred years later that the Dukes of Buccleuch began to reawaken and restore the landscape. It is a garden of land and water; avenues and vistas; rhythm and reflection.

The new landform at Boughton, responding to the 1724 pyramidal mound and the precise geometry of the early eighteenth century. The idea was to juxtapose an Orphean Hades with the Olympian Mount, designing the intervening ground plane to symbolize civilized life on Earth with the patterns of the classical Golden Section.

Although many of the landscapes we most enjoy are the results of eccentric and inspired individual patronage, few opportunities now arise to work with a really imaginative patron on this scale in a landscape of this importance. Institutions and committees are generally too cumbersome and diluted to commission really innovative work. The simple question on the hill was an intense moment and I am not sure what answer was expected, but one came to me in a flash. Rather than make a rival mount or competing structure, I replied: 'Why not go down rather than up?' I suggested inverting the pyramid across the river and digging a mirroring hole that descended the mount's 7 metres (23 feet) below the water table. Amazingly we went on from there.

BELOW The precise mathematical layout of Boughton in the 1720s, possibly by Charles Bridgeman. The mound and axial 'hurried over' run up through the centre of the drawing.

RIGHT The Orpheus landform inverts the 1724 truncated pyramid across the river.

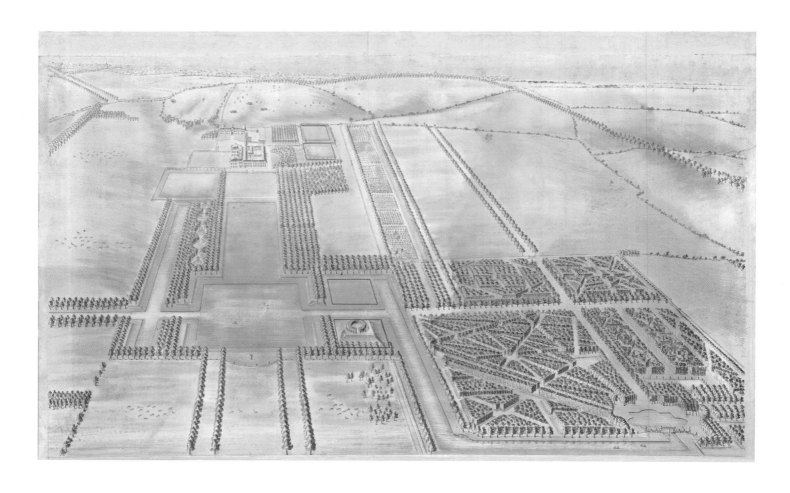

Two immediate challenges became apparent: hydrology and archaeology. Digging a 50 x 50 metre (165 x 165 foot) hole down seven metres (23 feet) beside a flowing river has some inherent problems. The house and garden are also listed as Grade I, so every millimetre of the project had to be checked for archaeological remains. We were fortunate in an exceptional team: Brian Dix on the archaeology, Miles Waterscapes on the very precise construction and Mott Macdonald on the engineering – all coordinated by the remarkable landscape manager at Boughton, Lance Goffort-Hall. After some initial nail chewing, the archaeological concerns calmed down. It turned out that the area had indeed been 'hurried over' and the remnants of a minor earlier parterre had been lost in dredging activity during the

previous century. The engineering issues too were resolved by a seam of finest blue clay beneath the surface, which meant that the landform could be constructed as a kind of reverse reservoir to keep the pressure of the ground water from bursting through. English Heritage and the local authority were exacting but very helpful, and the whole thing was built within a year of starting and opened in a classic English downpour.

The seventeenth/eighteenth-century layout of the Boughton landscape is based on the most precise geometry and mathematics. On studying the axial rhythm of squares within the wider geometry of the landscape, some interesting patterns and relationships emerged. The mount and empty rectangle of land across the river each form perfect Golden Rectangles, the

Charles Bridgeman was an expert in the use of the proportions of the Golden Section. It is interesting to superimpose Vitruvian Man on his design for Kensington Palace (TOP LEFT) and indeed on the combination of the mount and Orpheus (TOP RIGHT).

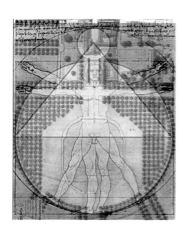
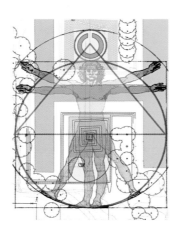

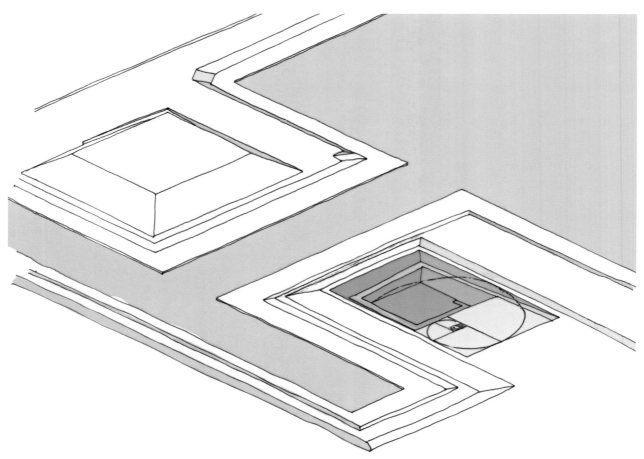

classic proportions observed by Hadrian, Vitruvius, da Vinci and Corbusier in creating harmony between man and geometry. Bridgeman was a keen observer of these rules and his designs for Kensington Palace Gardens, as well as Boughton, are revealing when Vitruvian man is superimposed on the plans.

The harmonic proportions are based on the perfect relationship between a square and a rectangle. Whenever a square is inserted into the Golden Rectangle, a rectangle of exactly the same proportions remains. The rectangle/square relationship can subdivide infinitely, creating a beautiful spiral as each of the squares' corners are connected. The Golden Section spiral is similar to the Fibonacci Series spiral, but the pattern is more precise, as it is based in geometric form rather than numerical

sequence. The geometry discovered in the existing garden has been a guiding principle for the inverted pyramid. The rhythm of squares is followed and linked by a spiral rill of water that then translates into a gentle grass path which descends to a square reflecting pool at the base of the inverted pyramid. Spring water from the source at the lily pond, half a mile away, bubbles up in the centre of the spiral and then flows down into the lower pool before returning to the river. As a final exploration of the perfect geometries, a polished 4 metre (13 foot) steel cube pops up into three dimensions on axis with the medieval pond. Its burnished surface glows with the setting sun.

The new design continues the materials of Boughton: grass, stone, oak and water. The grass slopes of the inverted pyramid

Although the Orpheus landform offers its
own contemporary drama, it has been
deliberately set low to respect the earlier
landscape and blend into the greater pattern.

match the mount in angle and character and the gentle grass ramp that spirals down to the lower pool is graded to 1 in 40. The reflecting pool is contained by the same oak as the canals to give a clean turf edge to the water. The Golden Section paths, rill and upper pool are cut by the local estate stonemasons to mark the pattern within the turf. The land between the inverted pyramid and the lily pond is being managed for the fritillaries and wildflowers that thrive there. The longer grass is mown into four squares of 60 metres (200 feet) that follow the centre line of the lily pond and create a subtle continuity of axial formality to connect the sequence of square spaces, from the upper lawn down to the mount. Specialized remote-controlled banks mowers enable the team of gardeners at Boughton to keep the entire grass and water landscape in crisp simplicity.

When you walk around the landscape, the new design is deliberately invisible, but drawing near to the mount, you catch sight of the gentle grass path that spirals down and through the pool of still water deep underground. The water reflects the sky, a little like an inverted James Turrell oculus, to create an Orphean Hades to complement the Olympian Mount. The earthwork came to be named after Orpheus to capture its descending form and as a place for music and contemplation. When Orpheus' wife, Eurydice, was killed by the bite of a serpent, he went down to the Underworld to bring her back. His songs were so beautiful that Hades finally agreed to allow Eurydice to return to the world of the living — until Orpheus doubted and looked back to check that she was really there.

Beneath all the mathematics and engineering, there is a special feeling at Boughton. The clarity and simplicity of the shapes work with shadows and reflections to make a huge landscape of planes of light that show the sky and space in a fresh way. Orpheus is a surprise. As you come to the lip of the landform, it opens as a vertiginous hole. The sides appear much steeper and the bottom much deeper than they really are. The grass path, however, is gentle as it unwinds along the sides of the pyramid. It is 250 metres (275 yards) long and takes some time to descend. As you go down the air gets stiller and the surface sounds disappear. It becomes quiet and contemplative. Then just as you are nearing the bottom, the square of water brings the sky into clear focus. The path continues to spiral down beneath the water, but there is a moment when you pause on the edge of the water, deep underground but surrounded by light.

For me that boundary between sky and earth or land and water is a magical pivot of existence. It does take you to a kind of Orphean dilemma; or perhaps to a place of connection with those you have lost who are still really a part of you and to that perplexing duality of being that can only be grasped through the senses and not fully understood by the mind. Orpheus is now a place for music, for art installations and for parties, but when you are alone there, it is a place to lose yourself in thought.

Franklin Farm, Hampshire.

HOME GROUND

Although I work all over the world, I have tried where possible to concentrate on projects within the narrow orbits of my studio in Richmond and our farm in Hampshire. It is easier to build a deeper relationship with the landscape, community and history of your home ground. The faces and stories become more familiar and your ability to interact spontaneously and continuously is helped by living on the spot.

Richmond is a dream of *rus in urbe*, Arcadia in the city. The combination of the river, the 9.5 square kilometre (2,360 acre) deer park and the thriving centre make it at once urban and yet surrounded and permeated by green open space. Richmond is a readily identifiable local community, but it is just fifteen minutes by train from the centre of London – a great recipe for sustainable urban life. And then the Hampshire downs are firmly home.

Our studio is on the top of Richmond Hill, high above the river and the flood plain and beside the Royal Park. Behind the house, I was able to reassemble the land and make a small walled garden. The main living accommodation on the first floor opens on to a roof terrace that overlooks Richmond Park. A big glass block table there doubles as a roof light for my desk below and is surrounded by copper planters in which grow vegetables and herbs.

On the ground floor the studio links to the walled garden, which catches the lunchtime sun. I worked with the sculptor Ben Barrell to design a big blue bench that five of us could sit on in the sunshine. It follows Ben's wonderful hydrodynamic lines and fortuitously mimics the shape of the sycamore helicopters that fall from the tree above.

The roof terrace above the studio in Richmond. The glass table doubles as the roof light for my desk.

BELOW Shallow waves of snowdrops advance on the studio from a car park of recycled blue glass.

RIGHT The bench by Ben Barrell was designed for us all to sit in the lunch-time sun.

The garden has a ceiling of orange-barked strawberry trees (*Arbutus* x *andrachnoides*), walls of deep blue ceanothus (*C. azureus* 'Concha') and a carpet of blue *Agapanthus africanus*. Apart from being a place for studio lunches, it is a garden to be looked down on from the roof terrace above. Bright blue recycled glass covers the parking area at one end, with eighty points of fibre-optic light hidden in the surface. The blue glass represents deep sea and then waves of Yorkshire fog, a grass, roll in before descending down periwinkle (*Vinca minor* 'Bowles') and rosemary (*Rosmarinus prostratus*) to the basement terrace.

Even in small suburban gardens the odd bit of land sculpting can work. Just 30 centimetre (1 foot) changes in elevation have turned a flat lawn into a series of waves. The crests are differentiated from the troughs by snowdrops, with alternating species of grass exaggerating the effect. Yorkshire fog is left to grow and flower on the crests and produces creamy waves that move with the wind, contrasting with the smooth green planes of mown grass.

FRANKLIN FARM
HAMPSHIRE

And so finally to the taproot. My grandfather first heard about Franklin Farm when it was about to be bulldozed to the ground and my parents were able to buy the ruined farm buildings and slowly rescue them from collapse. For nearly a thousand years there had been a consistent pattern of settlement on this land, owned and tenanted by Titchfield Abbey and then, after the dissolution of the monasteries, by the Earl of Southampton. Agricultural fortunes rose and fell up to the First World War when the loss of life left a number of the farms unmanned. Many holdings were then amalgamated and the farmhouses divided up to form labourers' cottages. After the Second World War a number of these houses were completely abandoned. Franklin Farm was one.

The farm sits on gentle downland that has been settled for a long time. There is a Bronze Age barrow on the ridge and, hidden under the furrowed brow, the remains of an ancient British village on the way to a group of Iron Age tumuli. We saw some of the treasures in Winchester Museum that had been excavated from the barrow and my passion was fired, though I was completely unaware that a 'barrow' was a burial mound rather than a wheelbarrow. Under all the brambles at Franklin Farm there was a dew pond dumped full of rusty milk churns, bicycles and wheelbarrows. As a seven-year old, I spent day after day secretly searching through broken wheelbarrows, sure that I would discover more jewels and make our fortune.

Franklin Farm is an old settlement on the Hampshire downs not far from the coast.

A sunken spiral curves out through the field to a small mound. From the top of the mound you can see Tennyson Down on the Isle of Wight.

the horizon. I planted 4 hectares (10 acres) of wood to follow the gentle contours of the land and cup around curious dimples in the surface. As the trees have grown up, the shadows now pick out the form of the valley and the dimples have been turned into dew ponds. As the canopy has closed, woodland flora has seeded itself, starting with vetches and crosswort and progressing to primroses, helleborines and orchids. The insects, birds and mammals have multiplied and the grim field of oilseed rape has reverted to a complex community of buzzing, singing and burrowing. The wood will be twenty years old this year and we have already started thinning and coppicing, not only for the hazel wattle but also to stoke the woodchip boiler that fuels all the buildings on the farm.

The design of the garden has been based on the two alignments of the buildings. The fifteenth-century house and cow byre are aligned north–south looking down the valley towards the sea, whereas the nineteenth-century barns splay a little on the east–west axis. Immediately beside the house is the old circular dew pond. Collection of rain and dew in dry chalk valleys was always very important. The circle of the pond and the gentle curving forms of the valley have led to a serpentine ha-ha and fence line. East of the house we cut an Archimedes spiral down into the chalk, curling in towards a sculpture by Simon Thomas. The spiral then rises up and unfolds out into the field to reverse direction and climb a small Golden Section spiral mound. I experimented on all these forms at home myself before risking them on clients. From the top of the mound you can just see to Tennyson Down on the Isle of Wight. My dog is buried in the mound and I will join him there one day.

The junction between garden and countryside is one of the most difficult tensions in design. The ha-ha, or sunken fence, was a great invention, allowing views out to grazing livestock without making a harsh division between field and garden. The lines of ha-has, fences and hedgerows are nevertheless extremely tricky. Brown was brilliant at curving his ha-has to follow the flow of the land, especially at Chilham Castle and Syon Park. On a smaller domestic scale the curves have to be a little more pronounced and exaggerated. Deliberate breaks in the curves for gates can help changes in arc and direction.

While the pond and valley set up a series of curves and circles around the house, the long line of nineteenth-century flint barns determined a more orthogonal grid. In the lee of the barns,

Although the place had been surrounded by ancient woodland, by the time we found it, all the trees had been cut down and the abandoned house and barns squatted rather forlornly on the edge of a huge and apparently flat, arable field. The spot nevertheless still had a profound atmosphere of peace and for us children it was heaven. In Middle English a 'franklin' was a free man rather than a serf and the farm was specially noted for being tenanted by a free man. The rent was a pound of cumin at Michaelmas. Some of that sense of calm independence seems to be an intrinsic part of the place.

Gradually the house was made habitable and a long series of experiments with the garden began. Twenty years ago we managed to buy back some of the farmland and I planted over four thousand trees to restore the enclosure and protection from the Channel winds. Today my partner and I now live here and we are breeding a herd of Longhorn cattle. We have unpicked the 1960s rescue work and rebuilt walls, cutting and weaving our own hazel for wattle and digging up our chalk for daub.

Restoring chalk meadows and planting woods is a slow but wonderful process. A bald arable field sprouts a bristle of tree tubes and then nothing seems to happen for a while, except that the voles and mice move into the tubes and the area becomes patrolled by barn owls. Then one spring green shoots appear out of the tubes and before you know it real trees start to break

we made a pair of walled gardens that are cut into the sloping land and bake in the sun, protected from the wind. I designed the first walled garden when I was fresh from Berkeley, using salvage from the Manchester Brewery archway. The intersecting rectangular lines are made from terracotta and the planting is of deep reds, blues and purples. The second garden is a contrast, using flint and pale white and yellow planting in a sunken grid. The garden gets the last of the evening sun and catches the rising moon from an old outdoor bathtub.

A vegetable garden and orchard are wrapped around the kitchen. The farmyard, chickens, turkeys and ducks are off to

The second walled garden of flint and brick with an old outdoor bath.

north-east in a second courtyard. Flint is everywhere. Each bed has to be sieved and the fields have to be picked of monster flint stones. So the walls, the paving and the ha-has are made from the ubiquitous rock. Flint is still something of a geological mystery but the current theory is that it is a sedimentary cryptocrystalline formation created by water flowing through chalk. When the flint is knapped, or broken in two, the halves open to a black glassy centre, surrounded by a white rim. Bound together in walls with lime mortar or in paving with crushed chalk, the flint produces a very tough black and white surface that reflects a silver light and glistens in rain or dew. Construction in flint is very particular

to the geology of parts of southern England and there is joy in discovering old techniques and inventing new uses for this very site-specific rock.

There is a sense of being a continuing part of 3,000 years of settlement here. The Saxon hearth became a chimney in 1620, but we still gather around the same fire in the evening, tend the woods, graze the downs and harvest water and vegetables in a way that this thin chalk soil can support. For all our technological advances, there are some fundamental relationships with the soil that persist. The tumuli have inspired new earthforms, the flint has shaped new paving and walling patterns, and the field and woodland boundaries have evolved with farming methods and view lines. But deep down, we are still a sequence of settlers cooperating with the land, cohabiting with wildlife and drawing inspiration from the spirit of the place.

Flint and chalk are everywhere, in the walls, in the paving and in every precious kilo of topsoil that you have to sieve and feed to grow anything.

INDEX

Page numbers in *italic* refer to captions

AUTHOR ACKNOWLEDGMENTS

The full title of this book should probably be Led by the Land and the People in it. There have been many people who have directly and indirectly helped me to write this book. My mother, my sister and Ilse Treurnicht gave me the courage to make the first leap and become a landscape architect. Ranunculus was a muddy stalwart through most of these projects and Pip has knocked into me a healthy sense of perspective on it all.

My professor at Berkeley, Michael Laurie, and my fellow classmates, especially Louise Mozingo and Mark Adams, helped to turn excited curiosity into determination. I am grateful to Richard Flenley, who gave me my first job as a landscape architect, and to the excellent people who have passed through my practice, starting with the irrepressible Marco Battaggia and continuing through Alex Evans, Eva Henze, Peter Wilder, John Goldwyn, Max Askew, Tessa Walliman Taylor, John Dawkins, Jeremy Rye, Chris Connor, Simon Rackham, Christina West and Grania Loughnan.

There are some particular people that I would also like to thank. When I first set up on my own, Mavis Batey and Gilly Drummond gave me tremendous support. Mavis taught me about the subtleties of landscape history and philosophy, and Gilly showed me how to manoeuvre the corridors of power to make things happen. Along the way I have had some great conversations with Laura Beatty, James Kidner, Tom and Caitlin Sargent, and Adam Nicolson, which ploughed questions and directions into my lumpy thoughts. John Nicoll showed amazing patience and perseverance in getting me to write the book. And lastly Rob Orford has been an invaluable guide through all my earthworks with his genius digger driver, Colin Mortlock.

Special acknowledgments are due on each of the projects I mention:
Solovki: The Prince of Wales's Business Leaders Forum, Susan Causey, Elizabeth White, Artyom Parshin and Brian Dix
Transylvania: The Mihai Eminescu Trust, The Prince of Wales's Charitable Foundation, Jessica Douglas Home, William Blacker and Nat Page
Thames Landscape Strategy: Sherban Cantecuzino, David Coleman, Sir David Attenborough, John Gummer, Jason Debney, Ken MacKenzie, Donna Clack, Jenny Pearce, Mavis Batey, David Lambert, Henrietta Buttery, Chris Sumner and Mike Dawson
Longwood Gardens: Paul Redman, Sharon Loving, Rodney Eason, Stu Appel, Alex Michaelis, FMG and Kate Donnelly

Villa La Pietra: New York University, Dr Robert Berne, Ellyn Toscano, Nick Dakin-Elliot, Lorenzo Nizzi Grifi and Rudy Rooms
Apothecaries' Garden: Dmitri Schvidkovsky, Sergei and Georgi Gevorkyan, Artyom Parshin and Alexi Retejum
Oxford Botanic Garden: The Friends of Oxford Botanic Garden, Timothy Walker and especially Louise Allen and Piers Newth
Chelsea Barracks: Quatari Diar, Jeremy Titchen, Michael Squire, Sir Jeremy Dixon and Edward Jones
Winchester water meadows: Jeff Hynam, John Wells, Robin Chute, Peter Wilson, Dr Rue Ekins and Graham Roberts
Shawford Park: Peter and Bettina Mallinson, Peter and Christian Douglas, Peter Glyn Jones and Bruce Guest
Heveningham Hall: Jon and Lois Hunt, Argus Gathorne-Hardy, Graham Broadhurst, Rowena Francombe, Grahame Sutherland, Peter Holborn and Anne Westover
V&A: John Madejski, Gwyn Miles, Stephen Doherty, Sir Mark Jones, Moira Gemmill, Jane Lawson, Steve Hyde and Sarah Drysdale
Hyde Park Corner: English Heritage, The Royal Parks, Westminster City Council, The Crown Estate, The Grosvenor Estate, The Royal Household, Transport for London, DCMS, CABE, Australian and New Zealand High Commissions, Philip Davies, John Barnes and Drew Bennellick
Hyde Abbey Garden: Friends of Hyde Abbey Garden, Winchester City Council, Hampshire Gardens Trust and especially Barbara Hall, Ken Qualmann, Dick Winney and Tracey Sheppard
City of London Cemetery: Corporation of the City of London, Ian Hussein, David Lambert and Margaret Cooke
Great Fosters: The Sutcliffe family, Richard Young and Russell Dixon
Holker Hall: Hugh, Grania and Lucy Cavendish, Duncan Peake, Yvonne Cannon, Mark Carroll and Tim Hatton
County Hall: Stuart Guest
Hurstbourne Park: Nick and Tal Fane
The Holt: Ted and Katherine Wake
Rotherfield Park: James, Judy, Arthur and Emily Scott
The King's Observatory: Robbie Brothers, Peter Riddington, Tanvir Hasan, Mike Broderick and Elizabeth Gent
Boughton House: The Duke and Duchess of Buccleuch, Lance Goffort Hall, Chris Sparrow, Rob Orford and Colin Mortlock

ILLUSTRATION ACKNOWLEDGMENTS

All the photographs are by Kim Wilkie and the drawings are copyright Kim Wilkie with the exception of the following:

Artyom Parshin pp12, 15, 45
Barbara Hall p94 top
Bruce Guest pp69, 70–71
Duke of Buccleuch p152
English Heritage p74 top
Grania Cavendish p126
Hampshire Wildlife Trust p60

Higher Perspective (www.ahigherperspective.co.uk) pp67, 135, 136, 139, 141, 151, 157, 165
Jonathan Buckley and Sarah Raven pp52–3, 56, 57
London Borough of Richmond upon Thames pp146, 147
Michael Squire and Partners p54
National Trust © NTPL/Andrew Butler p111
Pip Morrison p172 top
Private Collection p110 bottom
Robert Orford p75
Tate Britain © Tate, London 2011 p26 top
Winchester College pp62, 63